Bob Carlsen

Sacred Dust on Crowded Streets

Conversations with India

Order this book online at www.trafford.com
or email orders@trafford.com

Most Trafford titles are also available at major online book retailers.

Note for Librarians: A cataloguing record for this book is available from Library
and Archives Canada at www.collectionscanada.ca/amicus/index-e.html

Printed in Victoria, BC, Canada.

ISBN: 978-1-4269-2391-3

*Our mission is to efficiently provide the world's finest, most comprehensive book publishing
service, enabling every author to experience success. To find out how to publish your
book, your way, and have it available worldwide, visit us online at www.trafford.com*

Trafford rev. 3/02/2010

 www.trafford.com

North America & international
toll-free: 1 888 232 4444 (USA & Canada)
phone: 250 383 6864 ♦ fax: 812 355 4082

Sacred Dust on Crowded Streets

For Patti and Nicholas, whose love, support and inspiration made this adventure in India a reality;

Special thanks to the Missionary Sisters of Charity in Bangalore, and the orphans they care for; their smiles, dedication and love help me see the unwavering and sacred soul of India;

Contents

Preface   ix

Introduction - India in a Nutshell? Impossible!   1

"My Sister is Getting Married"   11

Charity in Calcutta   15

"What Country, sir?"   19

Take the Road, not the beach.   23

God in the Clouds   27

The Street Cobbler   31

Gandhi on Every Street Corner   37

An Orphanage in Bangalore   41

Dr. Bob   45

The Hero Bicycle   49

Banyan Tree Monkey Man   55

The Tailor   61

Life near the Jungle   67

The Jain Statue   71

Harish the Driver   77

My Daughter wants to Marry You!!!   85

Inspiration for the Journey   89

Forgiveness   93

A Taste of Paan   97

Give me ten Rupees!   101

Darjeeling Tea farms   107

An Indian Wedding   113

Do not commit nuisance!!   119

The Dance Village and Rock Pub 125

Some Reflections on Hinduism and Gandhi 129

The Jewel on the Hand 137

The Swami 141

A piece of Goa 147

Departure 151

Epilogue - Since My Return 155

Preface

ॐ

There is an India whose promise of the exotic lives deep inside us all. It is a land of surprises, magic, the sacred, the beautiful, the challenging – a place that is completely different, unique, and one of a kind. One cannot simply stand silent in the face of India's phenomenal history, tremendous temples, deep reverence for the holy, oppressive poverty and daily challenges. Visitors experience all of this in full measure, every day, when traveling in this magnetic land. A friend of mine told me that he had a headache for two weeks straight after arriving in India, as his brain could simply not catch up with the sensory bombardment of an Indian workday! India forces a reaction from all observers. You cannot hold your breath!

I have become completely enchanted by this magnificent country, whose daily "turn of the wheel" (the "chakra") unveils a kaleidoscope of sights, sounds, smells, thoughts, and superstitions. And yes, quite a bit of focus on the sacred.

I never expected to live or work there. Nor did I expect India to leave the deep and life changing impression on me that it has.

Why India?

Twenty years of legal practice in a multinational corporation has brought me to many international cities and shores. As is typical of most business travel, even to interesting places, one is generally only offered the opportunity for a long day in the office, perhaps a lunch or dinner outside the hotel with local contacts, and a night's sleep in a hotel bed that could be almost anywhere. The software industry, however, changed all that for me and put India, and certainly the city of Bangalore, on the technology map starting in the mid 1990s.

My company, a global leader in information technology and solutions, had been steadily investing and increasing the number of software developers in India shortly after the year 2000. As all multinational companies now know, Indian software developers possess excellent technical skills, speak English well, efficiently develop sophisticated software, de-bug programs, and assist with customer support in ways that are changing the IT industry. For my corporate client, this surge in human capital investment also drove another need, a need which up to that point had generally been overlooked, and could not easily be handled locally. That need was an expertise in software development law, and intellectual property matters generally. Neither the Indian IT curriculum, nor the legal profession in India as a whole, has historically required a need to focus on "intellectual property" as an academic subject. Indeed, prior to the current technology boom in India, the protection of the rights of authors, inventors and employers in software and technology was largely unnecessary as a legal matter. The market today is forcing that curriculum change in order to service the needs of local Indian software companies (which continue to sprout up daily!) seeking to protect their investments in a global economy. When I left for India in 2005, the need had hit a critical level for the software industry as increasing numbers of foreign software professionals were heading to India to manage and assist in this largest growing segment of the Indian economy.

Simply stated, most multinational technology companies licensing software to US-based customers must comply with the applicable laws of the United States, even when the software was written overseas by foreign nationals. Software litigation, usually in the form of copyright, patent or trade secret infringement (i.e., stealing someone else's work product, copying it, and distributing it) is a healthy area of dispute in US courts to say the least. Foreign software developers need to be trained on how to comply with US law to avoid legal problems for their multinational employers and customers in the US.

For example, many software developers in countries without deep technology experience view software which can be downloaded for "free" from the internet as...... well,........ "free!" Once I "click and accept," I can do whatever I want with the software that I just downloaded to my computer. In talking with many Indian software developers I would often hear, "Well, I followed the rules, I "accepted," by clicking the button, and now I can add this function to my own software to ship to my customer for next week's deadline." Alas...if the world of software were only so easy. In most circumstances, the button that was clicked on line was the "acceptance" of a software license, whose terms may have specifically prohibited the software developer from redistributing, or "shipping" the software to the customer for whom next week's deadline is fast approaching. The licenses may have also contained other restrictions, liabilities, and risks which would remain hidden in the absence of an educated developer or lawyer reviewing the license in advance. See the problem? Large companies need to educate their international development teams on software license compliance. Software developers in the IT industry, regardless of where they are located, need to understand when they can and cannot use someone else's software in their products. Complying with and understanding these licenses is just one way to avoid costly lawsuits, and other legal problems, for technology companies.

And so came the unexpected opportunity of a lifetime. After much family discussion, research and investigation on India, I ordered my first ever "one way" airplane ticket - for the purpose of actually moving to Bangalore, India in the fall of 2005. As John Lennon once sang - "Instant Karma's gonna get you...... gonna knock you off your feet!" Four years later, and I'm still trying to stand up straight without holding on to the handrail!

Bangalore is a city of over 6 million people in south India and sits on what is called the Deccan Plateau. Bangalore's relatively higher elevation on the Plateau has long given it the reputation of having a cooler, more moderate climate, with extensive gardens and a generally more forgiving monsoon season. Indian retirees, particularly those in the armed forces and government sector, have long made Bangalore a quiet retirement destination. Bangalore's long standing history as a British supply station (cantonment) under the days of the British Empire has bequeathed to modern India many lovely colonial bungalows, lush vegetation, the English language, and efficient railroads.

Few would have expected, however, the dramatic increase in technology firms, specifically, software companies in this part of the world! Real commercial change had come to Bangalore just before the year 2000, with Indian software developers moving in from all parts of the country, fueling job growth across the technology and services sector. This in turn increased the need generally for all kinds of labor - drivers, cooks, maids, tea sellers, and retailers. With its economy starting to take off, Bangalore decided to flex its muscles and officially changed its name to "Bengaluru" in 2006. This is the local language (called "Kannada") spelling and pronunciation of the ancient city. Several other cities started to feel their oats as well, and changed their names over the years. As Madras became Chennai, Bombay turned into Mumbai, and Calcutta became Kolkata, a new India began asserting itself as a technology and investment hub, and cutting its ties with the

British ruled India of the past. Having experienced India from the inside, I am delighted to see the relatively young independent India, a mere 60 years old, play by its own rules, and take pride in its own wonderful accomplishments. But do not be surprised to hear many people still refer to these cities by their "old" names. It costs money to change maps, books and stationary!

I found out quickly that you cannot just get off the plane and snap into a comfortable, well-oiled routine easily in India. My first priority was to get into my apartment, set up shop in my new "home" (which should have been easy since it was pre-furnished), and try to stay cool. That legendary elevation and those cool Deccan breezes didn't help me much initially until my blood started to thin out, and I lost 10 pounds sweating every day. I just wanted to get things organized on the work and personal front as soon as possible to achieve a sense of control. After two weeks, I wound up with a comfortable place to stay in the central part of town, both relatively close to work, and within walking distance of a food market, mall, a Christian church, and Bangalore's large and famous park, called Cubban Park. This last location would fortunately provide the incentive for many hours of weekend wanderings, as it is a geographical focal point in Bangalore that could serve as my "compass" when I got lost. And, oh boy, did I get lost.

I had arrived during the height of the Indian festival season in October. The two big holidays are Dewali, the Hindu festival of lights and fireworks, followed by Eid ul Fitr, the celebration marking the end of Ramadan and fasting for Muslims. So the initial plan at quickly arranging my personal life was delayed a few weeks until the vacationing locals got back to work. Indeed, the first several weeks in Bangalore had more than the normal amount of "welcome to India" frustration. Appointments with workers were missed and cheerfully dismissed with a "Sir, it is Dewali, no? "I could not get any appliances set up in my flat during that first week due to these festivals, and I was told that I would invalidate the warranty if I tried to plug them in myself!

Generally, the task of arranging an appointment went something like this:

"Hello Sir, yes Sir, I'll be there at 3 sir".......sorry sir, stuck in traffic....... See you at 5pm, Sir.... Then, a call at 8pm – "Sorry sir, I had a problem.......I will set up the washing machine tomorrow Sir!" I still remember sheepishly asking a colleague's wife to "throw in" some of my own 2 week-old laundry, including every pair of underwear that I had, while I waited for the set up of my own appliances at the end of holidays. Of course, the evening that "Mr. Appliance Set up Man with Full Warranty" could come over, I was out of town. Now I know why so many people wash their clothing in the river over the rocks!

My car was not delivered for about 3 weeks despite the fact that it had been ordered, and paid for, a month in advance. This had the unintended benefit of forcing me to walk around, use rickshaws, and throw myself into local traffic... boosting my confidence and helping me to realize that yes, there are in fact cows in the road, and drivers will let them freely and safely pass. How does a foreigner cross the road? Quick, follow that cow!

However, after this month long crash course on how things get done in India, I found that I began to have some relatively empty weekends that I could fill with walks around town, day trips and eventually longer sojourns in what I still consider to be the most amazing country on the planet. These wanderings followed no pattern. I would simply leave my apartment, making sure I had enough water, sunglasses and a hat, and then I'd turn right or left depending upon mood, the wind, the sound of some distant music, avoiding a car that I knew was trying to kill me, or as I noticed over time - perhaps the Spirit's gentle hand at my back?

So began my two year conversation with India – her people, landmarks, religions, languages, food, pastimes, her deep challenges, and reasons for optimism. I kept a photo journal during my time in Bangalore which I e-mailed weekly back to family and friends, providing short explanations on places and events......... and some visual proof that I was alive and..... Yes, indeed, thriving! This went on for my stay in India, and many recipients of these pictures told me that they were actually looking forward to the next email. One teacher said she was showing the pictures to her world studies class, along with my brief explanations. I got wonderful responses from my extended family and friends, and I began to think that documenting my trip was somehow useful and therapeutic for me, and others.

Stories and events from this two year conversation with India continue to invade my daily thoughts since I've returned. I now find that I am remembering more about what someone said, or the look on their face, or the sincerity of a gesture. The visual beauty of a temple, monument, or mountain remains fixed in my pictures, and I still treasure the memories they ignite. But while these visual images are worth thousands of words, as the saying goes, there are also some fascinating moments and impressions which my lens failed to capture.

I learned a great deal about travel generally during my stay in Bangalore. For example, its ability to shape our worldview, its frequent inconveniences and, perhaps, something of our responsibility as individuals privileged enough to see the world. It seems to me that short vacations often afford one the opportunity to see the beauty of a place, and get a refreshing change of scenery. At the other extreme, a lifetime of living in the same place can often dull one's senses to the ordinary tasks and events of day to day living, rendering them common and at times forgettable. Perhaps this is why so many of the world's great authors lived expatriate lives in order to describe their own countries and recreate the uniqueness of a place that only comes to mind when you are away long enough to miss it.

For me, two years of living and working in a foreign country seems to be just the right amount of time. It forces one to become a part of the local fabric, shop at the local markets and get to know the neighbors, and maybe even share a little gossip, while still seeing the place with the fresh and critical eyes of a visitor.

You simply cannot "hold your breath" for two years, trying to insulate yourself with bottled water and hand disinfectant, from the experience of really living in another place.

And who would want to? I decided to plunge into life in India with the excitement and curiosity of a graduate student who just won the greatest full paid fellowship to the University of their Choice! Imagine the chance to live in a country as diverse as the UN itself, where even my day to day work became an opportunity for study, learning and enrichment. And on the way I also caught tangible glimpses of God, Allah, Lord Krishna, and the Buddha at work in almost every turn, on almost every day. Not all my memories are sweet or happy. I did see poverty and a good deal of suffering. I saw lepers and crippled children on India's streets. I saw beggars whose lives were desperate, and abandoned children that made me cry. But I also saw struggle turn to determination, leading to success and achievement and beauty. I saw charity, people trying to make a difference, true generosity, and hospitality. I laughed a lot at my surroundings and myself, and got a chance to see how other cultures see the world, and Americans, and me. I made friends, had a chance to volunteer with Mother Teresa's nuns, saw Mt. Everest, I got to play guitar on stage with a band of Indian musicians, enjoyed a fulfilling worklife and colleagues,….. And much more. Pretty good for a technology lawyer!

I wore out and repaired several pair of shoes during these random jaunts. I had a tee shirt that became my favorite weekend attire. Printed on the front was a picture of an old shoe, with the words "Not all who wander are lost." I took to the streets without a map (occasionally unwise), and decided during those walks to inventory the amazing blessings given to me during this time in India…… I was given time to explore, I had two working legs, my health, and a lot of curiosity. I also soon learned that I was being lead down those "random" paths for a reason.

The stories that my pictures could not capture are the fruit of these cherished weekend walks. This is the conversation with

India that I want to share. I have an old pair of sandals from my time in Bangalore that should be thrown out – but I keep them, and always will, for only one reason. They still contain the sacred dust of those busy streets and the echoes of that conversation that I still hear everyday.

Jai Hind!!! (Go India) !!!

Bob "Raj" Carlsen,
Danbury, Connecticut. 2009.

Introduction - India in a Nutshell? Impossible!

For those with a limited knowledge of India, I would like to offer some of my own personal reflections and comments for context and background. This is not an academic history or societal study, but rather a review of some aspects of India's past and present that I found compelling, and which shaped my view of the country. While I was living in India, people at home would constantly ask me "Isn't India really dirty, and isn't there terrible poverty? How can you stand the heat? Are there really cows in the road? Are all the Indians super smart like they are in my son's class here in the US? "........... Where to begin? Are these even the right questions?

India is a vast country, as varied from North to South as can possibly be imagined. In speaking of India's people, it is difficult to even classify the billion-plus Indians into any ethnic group or common mindset, much less stereotype. Northern India borders the Himalayas, the source of the sacred river Ganges.

1

Since the Himalayas are largely in Nepal and Tibet/China, many Indians in the far north have lighter skin and facial features that are ethnically Oriental. There are a large numbers of Nepalese and Tibetan refugees in northern India, which contributes to the somewhat quieter mountain culture found in the North.

In contrast, southern India (from Mumbai on south) is generally flat, very agricultural, and ethnically and linguistically distinct. While North India generally speaks Hindi (derived from Sanskrit) or variations of Hindi, South India is marked by several major languages of completely different linguistic origin, with hundreds of dialects. English has increasingly become the common language for all of India, and most educated Indians speak English to a high degree. Between North and South, there have been centuries of influx of different colonial groups populating India, from the Mughal's (invading tribes from Persia who brought Islam to India), to the Portuguese and French who came for commercial and trading purposes. The British first set foot in India in approximately 1600 in search of cheaper spices, and other riches. Initially pursuing commercial benefit and trade, followed quickly by governance and dominion, the British stayed for 350 years, making India the "jewel in the crown of the British Empire." The British left India peacefully and in a hurry, granting India her independence in 1947 in one of the most fascinating episodes in world history.

There are still millions of isolated tribal peoples in different parts of India. There is some linguistic and DNA support for the southwestern part of India near Kerala being a source of the most ancient, deep migrations out of Africa during the dawn of civilization. Linguists have heard religious chanting among certain ancient communities in Kerala which are thought to resemble some of man's earliest attempts at human language. Regardless of linguistic differences, which often provide the best clues for migration, trade routes and the spread of culture, Indians come in all shapes, sizes and colors and embody physical characteristics from almost all civilizations. I began to realize this as I was going to breakfast on my first day in Bangalore. I was being served coffee by an attractive Oriental- looking woman, who I assumed emigrated from Thailand or Korea. She told me that, in fact, her family had been in India for over a hundred years, and they came from the region in the East of the country called Assam near the Burmese border. She herself grew up in Bangalore and spoke the local language in addition to 3 other Indian languages and English. By my second cup of coffee, I learned that most of my preconceptions about India would indeed need to be swept under the rug!

Religion does play a major role in Indian life, and India is truly a "spiritual" country in terms of priorities and focus, in large contrast to most of the West. The majority of Indians, about 83 percent, are Hindus. Hinduism is more a "way of life," or an outlook on life, then an organized set of religious practices or requirements. In Hinduism, the supreme God, Atman, can be represented by and through hundreds, if not thousands of other deities, many of which are appealed to for certain, specific needs or protections. The three major Hindu deities are Brahma, Vishnu and Shiva, who are respectively the deities of creation, preservation and destruction. These three gods embody the forces of cosmic creation, and the cycle of life and death.

Temples in India will generally honor one of the thousands of deities, depending upon the local favorite, with elaborate carvings and statues, colors, flames and decorations. Popular devotions to Ganesh (the elephant- headed boy deity who removes obstacles) and Hanuman (the monkey- headed deity known for strength and protection) abound everywhere, and such representations are often found on store signs, in shopping centers, and on cars. You could easily walk into Hanuman's electronic store and be greeted by a man named Krishna. Most Indian personal first names hearken back to a religious figure or deity from one of the epic religious texts. For Hindus, religion is very much externalized. Even events like the purchase of a new scooter or car could be memorialized with a small religious service, performed by a priest, to properly channel good luck, prosperity and blessings on the driver.

Hindus represent their gods in intricate detail in the form of statues, carvings, paintings, theatre and plays, and the arts. Hindu temples are thus very elaborate, almost alive, and are often a spectacular feast for the eyes. At a high level, Hinduism itself is fairly elastic when compared to the rules and prescriptions of Christianity or Judaism. Hinduism permits, and even encourages, as many forms of individual worship and practice as there are people. Why? Because the thrust of Hindu worship is the personal path to the divine. Its focus is on the individual finding god "in oneself" through renunciation, simple living, and non-violence. Hinduism does not require large communities of worship, or set worship times with posted schedules to conveniently accommodate the busy worshipper. Rather, Hinduism is flexible and encourages practices which bring one closer to finding god "inside" oneself. I recall reading a comparative discussion on Hinduism and Christianity, posing the question of "where is God?" The Christian would generally point to the sky, or upward, indicating heaven, whereas the Hindu would point to his or her heart.

For this reason, India still has many religious sages, or saddhus, who willingly renounce worldly possessions, sometimes even clothing, and in so emptying themselves of material concerns, leave more room for dependence on God alone. There is a certain resignation in Hinduism, when viewed on the surface, that your "lot" in life is fixed. It is determined by your birth (caste), and your choices of activities, including thoughts and deeds or "karma," which should correspond with your duty or "dharma" to live out the life and responsibilities which are appropriate to your station in life. Materialism takes a much less prominent role generally in Hindu thought. The perfect path is in emptying oneself of passions, vices and even some basic necessities to achieve virtue – because God is more easily revealed when life is uncluttered. While some see this as a "passive" religion, (you are what you are and you should live out your lot in life faithfully without seeking to climb the ladder), current Indian society is clearly on the move, and anything but passive. India is struggling, as are many traditional Asian countries, with finding that balance between increasing wealth, goods, and Western influence, and the preservation of traditional values and India's historical spiritual core.

India's second major religion is Islam, brought by the Moghul conquerors in around the 9th century. Islam, a monotheistic religion like Christianity or Judaism (all three of which believe that Abraham was the "father" of their religion) is shared by around 15% of the population, or 160 million Indians. India is in fact the second largest Muslim country in the world, next to Indonesia. Islam forbids representations of the Prophet Mohammed (who literally transcribed Allah's words from the mouth of the angel Gabriel to form the Koran), and thus Muslim mosques tend to be sparse buildings, functional only for prayer, and without decoration or statues. Muslims do not seek to "translate" their faith through epics, statues, or physical and tangible media. The life of the Prophet and the Koran are viewed as the only and adequate sacred examples of Islam and little else is needed to inform the basic tenets of the religion. In fact, "Islam" roughly translates into "one who surrenders," and thus there is at least on the surface a strong distinction between the flexibility of Hindu worship, and the relative rigidity of Islam.

As I read Indian history, my impression is that there has been general coexistence between the majority religion of Hinduism, and the strong minority faith of Islam. Centuries of being forced to struggle together in communities to make a living tends to breed cooperation, and understanding. That is not to say that Indian history is without some very serious uprisings and conflicts stemming from religious differences, or political differences fueled by religion. But the more recent religious tension between Hindus and Moslems in India stems more from the "Partition" of India in 1947, which formed India and Pakistan, then from core religious differences in my view. The British needed an expedited way to quickly exit the country, in the face of almost universal opposition to their rule and their inability to effectively govern a people who, through the confidence provided to them largely by Gandhi, were ready to govern themselves. However, the Moslem population was extremely afraid of becoming a politically weak minority group, governed by an overwhelming Hindu majority without the British to arbitrate disputes. To accommodate this, the British took out their maps and pencils, and divided the Indian subcontinent into India, and Pakistan / East Pakistan (now Bangladesh). These latter two were to be peopled by India's Muslims; according to the British view that peaceful transition would only come about if the division of India's masses into the two new nations was based on religion. While this likely appeased the Indian Muslim community initially, history has shown time and time again that such divisions based on religion are always a recipe for religious tension.

Other religions in India include many forms and rites of Christianity (perhaps 3% of the population), Buddhism (born in India and spread to southeast Asia), Jainism (a Hindu-like belief in strict non-violence), Sikhism (Sikhs are usually distinguished by their turbans and have as their spiritual center the Golden Temple in Amritsar, Punjab), as well as many others. While all of these groups add to the diverse kaleidoscope that is India, what fascinated me most was the relative ability of so many different people to get along in a place that is hot, crowded, and still largely poor.

I mention religion extensively because spirituality, in whatever form, is externalized far more in India then in the West. When I arrived, I thought that my view of peaceful gurus in lotus positions was the wishful thinking of westerners seeking to reclaim an Eden lost to Christians who had violently waged war through the centuries. But in my personal experience, I found spirituality and a commitment to holiness and correct living, to be a goal that people really wanted to attain in their lives generally in India, regardless of belief. At a high level, while the West generally has focused on material wealth, economic achievement and military strength, it is largely true that India has focused quite a bit more on the "Inner self". This is likely one reason why sparkling streets and well manicured developments are less important in most of India, at least historically. Cows do freely roam the streets in India, as the cow is revered in Hinduism as a "provider" and "sustainer" in this largely rural and agricultural land. Indeed, the accidental killing of a cow by a car or truck can provoke a very tense situation, particularly in a village or remote area. Such an act can be compounded if the driver is not a Hindu, as the accident could be viewed as having a religious motivation.

Thus, in India you see Hindu's spontaneously praying at temples, or stopping on the street to make an offering to a small statue of a deity placed somewhere in the middle of a commercial center. For equal measure on the Muslim side, one is reminded of the spiritual "higher calling" all day long as the Muslim call to prayer is loudly and emphatically intoned five times a day throughout the land. I think the call to prayer was likely the first sound I heard at about 4:45am upon waking up on my first day in Bangalore after the long trip from the US. I remain absolutely fascinated by these public religious intonations in a huge, spiritual democracy like India.

Politically, India is the largest democracy in the world! I think the fact that India has a truly functional democracy – with active debate on most every subject - is likely attributable to the historical melting pot which forced the peoples of the Indian subcontinent to absorb so many external influences and religions over the centuries. In addition, centuries of British rule, and the parliamentary proceedings which Indians learned about, even if they could not participate in them directly until near the end of colonial rule, clearly contributed to a respect for debate and argument. The politics of India have largely been dominated by the Congress Party, the party which Mahatma Gandhi helped found in the early 1900's, and which continued to rule India through Jawarhalal Nehru (India's first prime minister), the regime of the Gandhi's (Indira and her son Rajiv, – no relation to Mahatma Gandhi) and still today. The Congress Party, originally based on Gandhi's ideas, tends to embrace a more broadly inclusive view of religions and caste's, and counts Hindus, Muslims, and Christians as members. Naturally, there are other more focused political parties and coalitions, some of which represent a particular religious group, but India continues to survive with generally open elections and without any dictatorial intervention. For readers who really would like to better understand India's last one hundred years or so, including the fascinating time of the rise of Mahatma Gandhi, the last years of British rule, the Partition of India and Independence, I recommend "Freedom at Midnight," by Larry Collins and Dominique laPierre.

Economically, India has long been an agricultural nation, surviving on the precious rains of the monsoons, and the back breaking labor of its rural inhabitants. More recently, India's leading role in software, medical technology, IT services and increasingly, manufacturing, position India well for the future from an economic standpoint. Of all the emerging markets, India was the first to have an astronomy program and launch a rocket into space! While still largely agricultural, if India can focus on educating the poor, and in particular, prioritizing the importance of educating women, India's advantages, including the English language, rule of law, and democratic values, should provide the promise of a secure future as a major player in the world market. Poverty will exist in India, as in other parts of the world, as long as education is neglected in villages, and corruption is tolerated. But India can still do much to support the rights of women, and give families, and daughters, positive role models. In my outsider's view, Sonia Gandhi, the Italian born head of the Congress Party, could start this revolution by simple outreach to poor women in India, inspiring them to education through her leadership, and encouraging men in India to not be threatened by women who can contribute to the household and the nation.

What I have described above is certainly open to debate, and no doubt other observers with different backgrounds than my own will reach different conclusions on the same subjects. I simply wanted to set the stage for the conversations that I had with India, which follow below. While generalizations often miss the mark, the most remarkable characteristics I experienced in the Indians I interacted with included that rare quality of true hospitality, the genuine embrace of the phrase "the guest is god," coupled with a moral character, diligence in work and a friendly manner. I cannot forget the huge smiles or the gentle shake of the head which could mean "you are welcome"…or…. "I agree"… or simply, "all is well"! India, like all nations, has its problems, whether they be education, infrastructure, or the legacy issues of caste and religious tension. Much has been written on those topics and they should not be avoided if one wants a complete picture of this magnificent country.

In balance, I found a warm and friendly presence in the Indian people, unpredictability in day to day activities which forced me to "let go," and a window into God, my neighbor, and myself. I hope you enjoy these stories, and may they spark in you not only the desire to visit this unique land of beauty and contrasts, but perhaps also to begin your own conversation with God and neighbor, and your inner self.

"My Sister is Getting Married"

ॐ

The first adventure, or "initiation," for my visiting friends and family in Bangalore, India, was always a simple walk down a busy market street. This introductory lesson to a country with over a billion people showcased the chaos most foreigners experience as they vie for space on a road with cars, cows, people, rickshaws, hawkers, dogs, shops – and heat! In India, impromptu markets spring up everywhere. A bicycle or a patch of road becomes an instant display case for food and handiwork. Horns from cars and trucks blare constantly. The assault on the senses welcomes visitors to India better than any traditional string of garland or sweets!

All cities have their well established market centers. Commercial Street in Bangalore is such a place, drawing locals and occasional tourists to find clothing, plumbing supplies, electronics, and jewelry. Commercial Street and its surroundings have a high Muslim population, and its shops and stalls spread out over the watchful eye of the Jamma Masjid Mosque, which calls many of the shopkeepers to prayers 5 times a day. For North Americans, still trying to make sense of Islam in today's world, the first time you hear the call to prayer, particularly when close to the mosque, and see women scrambling around in full black "burqas," is a completely new and strange experience. You know that you are REALLY in a foreign land. Visitors are unsure of how to react to the sharp Arabic strains and high volume coming from the beautiful, but sparsely decorated mosque. That same call to prayer over time became a comfort to me, a reminder of our need to thank God frequently for the blessings in our lives. On the practical side, it also became an alarm clock!

During one particular stroll with jet lagged family members from the United States, we crossed near the mosque onto a side street, where exotic music could be heard, and children were running in and out of a hall. We were hot, thirsty and tired, and despite trying to convince my guests that we could safely drink from a tea stall, or snack on street food, they insisted on getting back to the apartment for a more "civilized" meal. As we started for home, a well dressed local man had stepped out of the hall for air, and sensing our curiosity, asked us where were from. We told him the US, and he seemed pleased to have curious foreigners wondering about the celebration that was taking place inside. He then asked us, "have you had your lunch?" and he proceeded to happily pull us inside to celebrate his own sister's wedding! Could you imagine doing the same at home with strangers from another country in the West?

This hospitable introduction to a land of hundreds of languages, dozens of religions, spectacular sights, clothing, food, and music proved to be a turning point for my newly arrived guests. Within minutes, we were greeted by many of the bride's male relatives as the women were celebrating separately upstairs per the Moslem custom at weddings. Steaming bowls of hot biryani (rice with chicken or mutton), plus delicious flat breads and other celebration food were placed in front of us on the many folding tables strewn about the large hall. With no silverware in sight, we began to eat with our hands as the other guests were doing, to the delight of my then 11 year old son! Soon pictures were being taken of us with members of the groom's family. If you looked upstairs, the young girls were running around, laughing, and furtively pointing to the foreigners below.

It was a truly wonderful scene of joy, activity and celebration. The food was delicious, our thirst was quenched, and we all silently sat in awe reflecting upon the hospitality shown to us by strangers. In India, the celebration is for all. We said our thanks and good byes and left with first hand knowledge of a culture which claims "The guest is god."

Charity in Calcutta

ॐ

I made a visit to Calcutta to see the home site of Mother Teresa's ministry. Her tomb is simply encased in stone and it sits inside the chapel where the sisters come to pray, just off a busy Calcutta street. Religious men and women, and pilgrims from all over the world gather daily to share in the intense spirituality of the Missionary Sisters of Charity as they perform their day to day tasks of caring for the poor and dying. The city of Calcutta, now renamed to Kolkata, was the historical seat of the British presence in India before they moved the capital to Dehli. Calcutta has impressive, European style boulevards and gardens, with large monuments and buildings, and shows two faces to the traveler. While buildings decay on the outside, with British era structures crumbling from heat and moisture, an active and determined swarm of people continue to survive with a spirit reflecting Mother Teresa's hope as they push the city and its almost 15 million inhabitants forward each day.

The mother house of the Sisters itself is clean and neatly maintained, with a grayish stone exterior. There are no gardens, or lawns to give the sisters some breathing room, rather, the building is right on the street, open to all that Calcutta and its inhabitants, including the millions of poor, have to deal with daily. The two sisters posted near the entrance at the time of my visit are confronted by hundreds of tourists and inquisitive locals each week. While they efficiently answer the many questions of the strangers who appear on their doorstep daily, they looked to me as if they would rather be off praying or directly helping the needy. Street shops, a stone's throw away down the busy street, cater to tourists seeking statues of Mother Teresa, photos, carvings, rosary beads, coffee cups – a true testament to the Indian spirit of commerce!

Upon leaving one such store with a tiny hand carved image of Blessed Teresa of Calcutta, I was quickly surrounded by several street children asking for money. In India, foreigners are obvious candidates for beggars, since the belief is that "gora," the Hindi slang for "pale" or foreigner, have money, and must give to charity as part of their Christian "duty." Sadly, most of the children begging on the street (or performing, dancing, tumbling, crying, etc) are part of larger groups organized by corrupt adults who force the children into begging under fear of punishment. The money you give to a child almost never goes to the child, their family, or even for their food for that matter. It is collected by the men who run the corrupt business which easily plays on the heartstrings of foreigners. Most locals will tell you NOT to give to street beggars generally, as that will simply provide more incentive for able bodied people not to work, and will perpetuate the begging cycle of families coming from villages to cities and living on the streets.

Some of the more clever kids try to overcome the reluctance or uneasiness of foreigners to give money to beggars by indicating with hand gestures that they are hungry and instead want food. As I stood outside the shop down the road from the Mother house, one little girl pulled my shirt and repeated "milk" in English, while pretending to rock a baby in her arms. She has learned that few people of good will would ever refuse to give some food to a hungry child. But oddly, she rejected the biscuits which I would carry in my backpack for just such an occasion. Instead, she and a little girl lead me to a small store nearby, where she pointed to a large box of powdered milk in the storefront window.

Feeling that this was a worthy and healthy substitute, and likely to go further then the biscuits anyway, I gladly went inside and paid the equivalent of $1 US dollar for a box of powdered milk, and gave it to the little girl. She and the others quickly scampered down the street, apparently happy and energetic, knowing that they had provided some sustenance for the family. I felt pleased as well, knowing that I hadn't simply given some money which would get turned over to a street goon. Goonda is the Indian slang word for thug.........and thug is the Hindi word for criminal!

I began to walk back towards the mother house, and while snapping a few pictures, I spotted the girls some distance away coming back to the same store where I had purchased the milk. The bigger girl went right into the store with the box of powdered milk, and a minute later came out with a bill of money in her hand, having sold it back to the shop keeper! I had been easily taken by these kids, like most foreigners are, but I couldn't feel angry. Actually I was impressed at the cleverness of the whole charade and its careful orchestration.

When I told one of the sisters about the incident later in the day, she looked at me a bit impatiently, and said "don't you know not to give these children anything? If they are really hungry, they will come to us and we will feed them. "Apparently, I had a lot to learn about the basics of charity in the streets of Calcutta!

The Mother House of the missionary order Mother Teresa
founded in Calcutta

"What Country, sir?"

ॐ

India has had foreigners in its midst for a long time. Three and a half centuries of the British "protectors," not to mention the arrival of the French, Portuguese, and the occasional Tibetan, has provided a steady flow of foreigners to India over the centuries. I was amazed, however, to encounter the high level of interest working class Indians have in knowing where individual tourists come from. My expectation before arriving in India was that hard working people, struggling every day to make a living, would not likely take any interest in someone like me, or would be simply to shy to ask.

I'm not sure if the interest is genuinely in the geography itself, or simply due to the fact that tourists have money, and in a poor country like India, tourists provide the rare opportunity for an unskilled laborer to get a tip or payment for doing something manual, like helping carry a tourist's bags. Many Americans have a strong sense of self reliance, and a bit of suspicion, which causes us to recoil a bit when someone offers to carry our luggage. We generally do these things ourselves, and in fact feel a bit apprehensive in parting with our goods, especially when five strangers are fighting for the right to carry them, and those bags contain all your belongings for the entire trip!

From the time you get off the plane in most Indian cities, or wherever there is an opportunity for a laborer to help you with anything, you are generally surrounded with offers for "help." While this was at times annoying, I learned over time to take it in stride. I would usually try to find someone to help me with bags when traveling or checking into a hotel because I felt I might be helping a family out by providing some money, even though I could do the task myself. The next question, as the bags were thrown hastily onto a cart, would typically be "what country, sir?"... and I soon realized that they were asking me where I was from.......... not where I had just landed!

The "what country" question also became a bit tiresome after about a month in Bangalore. I learned over time that the employees at my apartment building, the waiting drivers, cleaners and gardeners, really had no interest in getting any money from me. They were just making conversation, and were interested in a new face. Nevertheless, my immediate and misplaced fear of that "what country" question was that it would be followed, almost certainly, by a request for money, or for the opportunity to perform a service which I didn't solicit, or want. Occasionally, just to vindicate myself, I would answer with the wrong country, and say something absurd, like "China," or respond in a language other then English, which would usually stop the inquirer from pressing further. Sometimes these silly comments would get a shrug or a smile, which usually made me laugh at myself. I did learn over time that the natural friendliness of the people around me, who meant no malice and were simply interested in learning more about my background, was really worth the two minutes it might cost me to engage in the same line of questioning day after day. In fact, I am grateful for the patience and openness of heart shown to me, a newly arrived guest in India, which has helped me focus on patience and openness since I've returned. It is just another example of the good Lord viewing us as a work in progress. Still, it could get tiresome at times!

I attended mass in a small chapel run by some cloistered Carmelite nuns near my apartment. At 7am in my part of Bangalore, the streets were still quiet, and other then avoiding stepping on or near the ubiquitous street dogs, the walk to mass was peaceful, and I could actually look around, listen, and take in the new day. One morning, after leaving mass around 7:30am, I started to walk back to my apartment. By now the streets were coming to life. Horns were honking, busses were barreling down the road with people hanging off the sides, and rickshaws were buzzing all around as people got ready for work. The calm of the early morning was over, and my tension level, despite the peace and coolness of the stone chapel I had just left, was on the rise.

I could hear a motorcycle speed up behind me. I stepped further on to the sidewalk to make way for it, but it seemed to be following me, giving me little room to maneuver on the already crowded street. I was really annoyed as the motorcycle then actually caught up with me, then slowed down entirely, forcing me to stop on the road. The driver was dressed in a ski hat, and winter jacket (which always amazed me, as I was generally sweating most of the time in India), and with a huge smile asked me "where are you from?" Great, I thought…. Does the 'what country" routine really have to start this early, and in the middle of a crowded street?

I was a bit short of temper at this point, as I felt that I was close to getting run over. I shot back "where do YOU live?" The driver shut off his scooter, pulled off his hat, and with a big smile, said, "at the Bishop's house!" It was the priest who had just said mass at the chapel, from whom I had just received communion and offered a sign of peace. Embarrassed at my very terse and sharp response, I quickly sought to remedy the situation by telling him not only where I lived, but where I worked, how I liked India, how surprised I was with the large number of churches in Bangalore, etc. He offered his hand, welcomed me, and started his engine. He told me he was in a bit of a hurry and had to get off to the school where he was teaching, leaving me standing foolishly at the side of the road.

I learned to be a little more open, patient and welcoming of others that day. After all, I was the guest in India.

Take the Road,
not the beach.

ॐ

Goa is a small province in India on the Arabian Sea that is quite different from the rest of the country. Historically, it was occupied by the Portuguese until around 1961, when, 14 years after India's independence from the British, the Indian army peacefully nudged the Portuguese authorities out of the country. There are other spots of European influence which remain in India, notably Pondicherry, on the Indian Ocean, where the French similarly held sway for centuries. Both places, because of the European influence, have lots of Christian churches, and European colonial architecture. In both Goa and Pondicherry there is a wonderfully exotic mixture of Hinduism, Islam and Christianity, with exceptional food varieties and scenic beaches.

Goa in particular has been a favorite tourist spot for Westerners over the years. Its beaches are well kept during the tourist season from October to March (following the heat and rain of the monsoon season) and are lined with hundreds of beach shacks selling delicious seafood, kebabs, cold beer or fresh lime soda. As local prices are a fraction of what you would pay at a Mediterranean beach, charter planes roll into Goa with sun starved "gora" (foreigners) during this time. Local merchants really hustle to earn money during tourist season, putting out lounge chairs, offering to bring you snacks and drinks, or offering a parasailing adventure or taxi tour. Of course, there are thousands of beach walking merchants as well, generally clever, well spoken women hawking jewelry, tee shirts, trinkets, and handicrafts who have learned appropriate phrases in whatever language seems to predominate on that part of the beach during that particular tourist season. I met Indian beach merchants who could hold basic conversations in Russian, Finnish, Swedish and English, all in an effort to out do their competitors selling the same goods. Goa also had a reputation for a hippie culture in the 70's, and the presence of vacationing European foreigners in bikinis contrasts sharply with the generally conservative dress code of the locals. While I do recall seeing Indian women wade waist high into the sea on rare occasion, they were generally fully dressed in salwar chameez, or sweat suits!

I got a "promotional" email one day to stay at a nice, but heavily discounted, Goa resort in May after the tourist season had ended. I thought it would be a great way to get away from Bangalore's noise, and sit on the beach with a stack of books, meditate, and explore this fascinating land where many of the people have surnames like Fernandes, Gomes and D'Sousa. I had heard that some old timers, in the northern villages, still spoke Portuguese, or at least mixed it with the local "Konkini" dialect of Goa. However, after all I had heard about Goa, I was pretty shocked to find the beaches largely empty when I arrived, except for local fishermen and some odd merchants. Most of the shacks had shut down, and the pre-monsoon seas were beginning to churn. The skies were gray and drizzly, but it was warm, and I was happy to simply walk the beach quietly, alone, and stare out at the sea or read.

One morning, I got up early and wandered north on the beach in Cavalossim, off the hotel grounds and onto a part of the beach that was completely still, with no sign of life whatsoever. Not a boat or another morning walker, nor even a fisherman's hut in the brush opposite the sea, broke the straight line of sand and surf. After some time, I could see a lone dog coming out of the brush towards the water. It stopped, turned towards me, and began to bark at a run in my direction. I am not a big fan of stray dogs, no matter where they are, but I had heard stories in India of how packs of mangy, stray dogs had attacked and killed several children in Bangalore. I wasn't really worried until several more dogs came out of the brush, barking, and heading now directly towards me. I began to move up to the wooded area in the hopes of finding a stick or something to keep these dogs at bay, but by the time I got near the trees, there were about 15 dogs, hungry, skinny and dirty, starting to circle.

Apparently during the tourist season, the dogs are able to find scraps of food, garbage and enough to survive. However, when the beach shuts down for the monsoon season, the dogs again get malnourished, sick and desperate for food. I was quickly surrounded, and really had no alternative but to pray. The dogs were closing in, about 20 feet away, and all I had was a small stick. I was wondering if I should just dash for the ocean and swim out, but of course the dogs would be there when I returned.

I soon heard a man's voice amidst the barking. He was shouting at the dogs, and he held a large oar in his hand. He emerged from the woods, an answer to a prayer, and began swinging at the dogs, although not hitting them. He scared the dogs away with the oar and his shouts, motioning for me to go to the path in the trees from which he came. I did, and soon after he joined me. He was dressed in a dhoti (the colorful Indian short skirt that men wrap around their mid section), was bare chested, and had obviously just been awakened by the barking as it was still early. His hut was a little further in the woods, and he smiled when we arrived. His wife was starting a fire and was making tea.

I thanked him profusely, in English and Portuguese and Hindi (not really knowing anything of the local language), and he just smiled at me, and offered me some tea. I wanted to give him some money, but he just shook his head. On the wall of his hut was a picture of the Hindu deity Ganesh, the elephant headed boy god, revered throughout India as the facilitator, the god who "removes obstacles." There was also a cross on the wall.

I marvel at how I was delivered from a pack of hungry dogs, while praying to my Christian God, by a Hindu who puts his faith in Ganesh. As I discovered so many times, Indian hospitality came to the rescue of the foreigner. Months later, I was given a tee shirt by a friend which reads, "God is too big to fit into one religion." On that shirt was the Crescent of Islam, a small Ganesh, a Christian Cross, Buddhist "circle of life" and Jewish Star of David. This shirt has sharpened my view of brotherhood in a troubled world. It clearly saved me one May morning from an uncertain outcome on a beach in Goa.

After our tea, he told me to take the road back to my hotel, and not to walk on the beach any more because of the dogs. The rest of my day was spent on my balcony!

God in the Clouds

ॐ

Darjeeling is a magical and beautiful town, referred to locally as a "hill station." Hill stations are all over India, and they are generally cooler spots throughout the country where the British set up shop to escape India's heat during the warmest months. Darjeeling sits on the northern perimeter of the state of West Bengal, and is literally on the border of Nepal, and several hours drive from the exotic Tibetan landscape of Sikkim to the north, and the more remote Bhutan to the east. Tea plantations are all over Darjeeling's mountains and its people are an exotic blend of Indians, Nepali's, Tibetans, and Bhutanese, living under the Himalayan snow covered peak of Kanchenjunga, India's largest mountain, at over 28,000 feet. Darjeeling is the gateway to the Himalayas, and Tibetan culture. In the crisp and clear air of November and December, the most incredible snow-whipped, jagged mountains point upwards to the heavens. Visitors here feel quite small against this backdrop. Perhaps this is to let us know our place in the scheme of things. God gives us places like

Darjeeling to show us His love for us. I have never been to a more peaceful, spiritual and beautiful place.

The pace of life is quite a bit slower in Darjeeling when compared to the rest of India. The roads are generally narrow and built to accommodate the hills, which divide the town into the upper part, and the lower part. Buddhist monasteries and monks of all ages in flowing robes wander around, ringing peaceful prayer bells. Beautifully inscribed and colorful flags send prayers by the thousands to be carried off by the winds. Small Hindu temples spring up almost everywhere. There is always a sound of wind and bells, and chimes, creating a soothing blanket of peacefulness around the hills.

Nuns from Ireland established the Loreto Convent in Darjeeling over a century ago. It was on a trip returning from this convent in Darjeeling and back to Calcutta that Mother Teresa decided to found a new order of nuns, whose mission would be, and still is, total devotion to the poor. A Japanese peace pagoda brings people of all faiths to its worship center, where drumming and chanting sends out a calming message of unity to the hills. For a westerner, this place is the mystical Shangri La. Tibetan momos (chicken or vegetable filled dumplings), sumptuous breads, and butter tea provide inexpensive, hearty and delicious meals. You are more likely to hear Nepali, or Tibetan spoken in Darjeeling then Bengali, and the confluence of cultures produces an attractive, elegant, hospitable, and spiritual local populace.

One of the best days of my life started with an early morning climb to see Kanchenjunga in the morning sun. The snow was whipping off the top in the cold morning winds, and I had a warm cup of sweet tea from a local tea stall. Tibetan women in their colorful skirts accompanied men in reciting mantras and breathing exercises as they faced the awakening mountain. Sitting on a bench and watching the mountain come alive; you could hear the most ancient sanskrit word..... "om".........nasally droned as "oooooommmmmm" by dozens of people performing their morning mantra of prayers. Some bowed and prayed, some exercised with yoga, some ran along the paved walkway which overlooked the Himalayas. All was alive and yet peaceful. The kids at the Himalyan School for Tibetans in Darjeeling began to arrive in uniform. Many of them would stop at a statue and pray, silently looking at the mountains which pointed to the heavens.

These people were starting their day with prayer and thanksgiving. Many were poor, some no doubt in ill health, and struggling. But they had hope in the new day, and would not miss the early morning to thank God for his blessings.

I took a big gulp of that scene back with me. On cold mornings I close my eyes and I can feel the crisp Himalayan air, and the soft humming of 'oooommmm"!

A couple in Darjeeling

The Street Cobbler

ॐ

In India there are people engaged in every conceivable service and sale of goods. This in and of itself is not remarkable. What is fascinating is that the services are targeted at different economic levels of society. For example, wealthy people might have their own maid employed for washing, drying and ironing. Middle income people might have their own iron to press their clothes. Poorer people in India might bring a shirt to an ironing stall on the street, where clothes would be pressed very cheaply by a man with a mound of wrinkled clothes next to him and an old fashioned "iron" actually heated by burning wood. He might be flanked by another man cutting hair, and still another mending clothes on a stool. These workers would all be lined up on the street, near a bus stop or other busy spot to attract customers. Their days seem to pass slowly, and few of their faces revealed the kind of stress that many office workers in the West carry as their daily burden.

I am still amazed at how industrious Indians are in meeting the needs of their fellow countrymen. In the West, we are used to attending physical store locations, or shopping by internet, and getting in cars to drive to malls to buy our goods and procure services like clothing alterations or dry cleaning. In the West, having someone perform a service is generally expensive. We talk about things being "hand made"...... and thus of better quality. But in India, opportunity knocks where the people are, and where the hands are working..... and where the need is. Generally, a person who has any chance of making a few rupees for the day needs to be out on the street!

The street scene always fascinates me. On many a corner street in Bangalore you can find a couple of people cooking rice and dal (protein rich lentils) in large pots. This would be served with some naan (flat bread) and maybe a vegetable dish on metal plates for 20 Rupees, or less. Thus, a hot meal could be procured by a driver or perhaps a laborer for about 40 US cents. One would see 30 people lined up to get this sort of meal on streets in every city in India. Next door might be a man on a bicycle, from which would hang 30 fresh coconuts all securely tied to the bicycle which became his makeshift store front. The man would cut the coconuts open for his customers, right on the street or wherever you stopped him. He would provide a straw, and you would have wonderful, fresh coconut water to sip with a friend. When you finished, he would deftly split the husk so that you could get the meat out of the coconut if you wanted. This transaction might cost 10 cents. Barbers cut hair outside on the street for seventy five cents, using the same comb and scissors from one patron to the next. All manner of small tables provide sweets for pennies, a liter of chilled water for 20 cents, (or a cup of water from a communal jar for 3 cents) and most importantly, cups of sweet chai (tea) drunk by all, in hot and cold weather.

Of great interest to me were the street cobblers. In fixing and repairing shoes, they would generally squat cross legged inside wooden boxes the size of closet, set up in an advantageous location near lots of walking traffic. The cobbler box might have wheels to be moved around as demand or whim dictated. In India, it is my experience that shoes are viewed as almost completely utilitarian objects, with very little fashion value except among the wealthy or in the entertainment industry. Sandals or chappals, are most common, and are worn by all. They are inexpensive, breathable, made of simple leather, and slip on and off easily. The streets in India are dirty, and people universally remove their shoes when entering homes, places of worship, and even workshops or offices. Thus, since the shoes get dirty through wear, and wear out easily on rock, dirt and cement, finding a cheap way to repair shoes, which will just get dirty and broken again, is important!

The cobbler or shoe maker is historically a low caste Hindu, referred to by many as an "untouchable," because he works with the skin (leather) of the dead cow. This job is considered unclean by many and too low for a person of higher birth. The caste system in India developed and evolved over thousands of years, and was generally viewed as a means for the division of labor. At the top of the caste system were the priests, or Brahmins, and at the lowest end would be those that dealt with dead bodies, latrines, and other "unclean" roles. Merchants and warriors would be in the middle. Thus, the term "untouchable" came to refer to those engaged in unclean labors. Gandhi, and other activists of the 20th century like Dr. Ambedkar, struggled hard to remove "untouchability" from Hindu daily life. Gandhi did this by forcing even his own followers to clean latrines. He also got rid of the word "untouchable", choosing instead to call these workers, who had been discriminated against for centuries, "harijans", or Children of God. Dr. Ambedkar chose a different path, leading millions of untouchables away from Hinduism to embrace Buddhism, with its strong emphasis on the value and equality of all life. I don't think I ever passed a cobbler stall without viewing a garlanded picture of Dr. Ambedkar, with his thick eye glasses and round face prominently displayed. He must be the patron saint of cobblers in India!

However, the necessity of the cobbler was quite obvious as people would line up six deep to have a shoe strap re-attached, or a sole repaired. A good cobbler would have leather scraps of all sorts on hand, complete with stitching materials, strong nails to puncture leather and rubber, and glues to re-attach a rubber sole or additional sole reinforcement. All of this, and the cobbler himself, would generally fit into the portable cobbler closet!

One day I decided to stop at the local cobbler on my street, Cunningham Road, in Bangalore. The sole of a pair of walking shoes had cracked after a year of Indian heat and broken sidewalks, and I thought the experience of getting the shoes fixed by a street cobbler would be both interesting and inexpensive. I sat barefoot in a chair while he deftly and enthusiastically glued the crack together, then put a rubber patch on the outside, and then stitched the patch to the sole. I was impressed with the work, and to top it off, he shined both my shoes. Although he spoke Kannada, the local language of the state of Karnataka, he understood basic Hindi. The smiles and few Hindi words I could exchange lead him to believe that I was satisfied with the 20 minutes of work. In fact, there was an impatient line of about 4 people behind me, all wearing their broken sandals, and looking for a quick repair.

When I asked him "kitne" ("how much," in Hindi), he said "200 rupees" in English, an amount that was approximately $4 to $5 US dollars. Knowing the cost of shoe repair in the US, and the fact that I really enjoyed the experience, and really liked the shoes, I was only too happy to pay it. But the man in line behind me began to protest, in the Kannada language, and became quite agitated in rebuking the cobbler for overcharging me. The man, now in broken English, was both yelling at the cobbler and explaining to me that this job should be no more then 50 Rupees (a little more then a US dollar)! He proceeded to explain to me that because I was a foreigner, and likely didn't know any better, the cobbler was taking advantage of me. The cobbler became very upset, shouting back at the man, because, in fact, I would have been willing to pay the higher amount, had the well intentioned patron not intervened. The others in line began to berate the cobbler as well (street arguments always draw on-lookers in India, with people actually taking sides!) and I really began to be un-easy about the whole situation. Of course I didn't want to be taken advantage of, but I truly felt that I had received value which was worth the amount charged.

I thanked the man on the line behind me who was only looking out for my interest. I subsequently found out that I was indeed overcharged, but I decided to pay the cobbler the 200 Rupees because I was satisfied, and frankly, hadn't asked him for the price in advance. I handed the money somewhat furtively to the cobbler, to avoid the scene escalating further, and I walked away quickly. I will say that I was delighted to again wear those shoes which logged many miles on Bangalore streets!!

Almost every day for the next year, I passed the same cobbler in his stand, at the same place, and usually at the same time of day. And, almost every day, he put his hands together in the Hindu greeting of "Namaste" as I passed, whether I was alone or with friends. He smiled at me, and occasionally would glance down at my shoes and point to them to see if his handiwork was still holding up. He took pride in his work.

I felt that this daily blessing from the "untouchable" street cobbler was worth every rupee I had paid, and then some.

Gandhi on Every Street Corner

ॐ

The name and face of Mahatma Gandhi is emblazoned throughout the cities, streets and villages of India. Every city has its "Mahatma Gandhi Road" (or simply "MG Road"), which is typically a main commercial road in the town. Every city has some collection of statues, parks and other pavilions or "bhavans" to commemorate the deeds and ideals of the Father of the Nation. The cottage industry shops, which promote local handicrafts and "khadi" (the homespun cloth which Gandhi advocated as part of his non-violent protest against British occupation) sport large signs with the smiling face and bald head of "Bapu-ji", as he is affectionately known in India. Schools and institutes are named for the Mahatma, sites throughout the country where Gandhi and his followers worshipped are generally commemorated with a marker, and perhaps most ironically, Gandhi's face is on the currency of every rupee note in India!

But what about Gandhi's ideals? Do they still impact the mindset of average Indians today? While he is still revered by many, and public holidays commemorate his birthday in India, I was shocked, when living in India, to hear some younger people revile Gandhi as a mere politician, a sell out to the Muslim cause, and a weak leader that put India, in their view, on a 40 year course of non-engagement and poverty. While Gandhi's steadfast dedication to an India shared by all Indians and all religions ultimately lead to the British decision to quit India in 1947, Gandhi's ecumenical dedication to Hindu and Moslem brotherhood was also the reason for his assassination by a Hindu extremist. In an age of nationalism and superpowers, the concepts of non-violence, tolerance and self restraint continue to be at odds with progress in a global economy.

I had the opportunity to see some of this dialog unfold while I was in Bangalore. A movie, "Lage Raho Munna Bhai" (Brother Munna Returns!) was a very popular Hindi film at the time, and it re-opened the debate on "Gandhi-giri," or living out Gandhi's ideals. The movie is set in the scrappy, survival of the fittest city of Mumbai, formerly Bombay. In the film, a confirmed tough guy, Munna Bhai, (Brother Munna) makes his living kicking legitimate owners out of their homes through extortion and threats of violence. He works for the local mafia and is essentially corrupt and dishonest. He wins a contest to date an attractive female radio personality by calling into the station and correctly answering questions and facts about Gandhi's life. Of course, he had kidnapped several professors of history to feed him with the right answers, but for Munna, the end justified the means. When he finally meets the beautiful radio announcer, Munna pretends to be a history professor, and she is so impressed with his factual knowledge that she wants him to lecture on Gandhi and his ideals at a local old folks home, where her father is staying. Not wanting to be found out as a fraud, which would cause him to lose the girl has already fallen in love with, Munna has no choice but to actually study Gandhi's life and ideals to prepare for the lecture.

During the course of his study, the likeness of the Mahatma begins to appear to Munna at random, urging him on to a life of truthfulness, purpose, honesty and real compassion. However, no one else can see these apparitions. For Gandhi, "satya" or Truth is more important then earthly goals, and in fact, Munna learns that he can achieve nothing without a pure heart, right intentions and by embracing the truth. Ultimately, by confronting the hypocrisy and evil in his life and making positive changes, he begins to turn the city of Mumbai around, person by person, to the compassionate and truthful society that Gandhi envisioned. By exposing the evil in the system, and making the evil doer see their own actions as wrong, the people of Mumbai are transformed. At one point, Munna despairs, telling Gandhi's image that he simply cannot live up to Gandhi's ideals. Gandhi then tells him, and all of India, to tear down his statues, take his face off the currency, rip his name off signs…and only remember him in their hearts. The movie was both entertaining and uplifting! Lively debate ensued in the national press around 2005 and 2006, about whether a return to Gandhian thought could lift India out of corruption, and ultimately, lead to both economic and spiritual progress.

For my part, the India that I saw was largely tolerant and embracing of diversity. Politically, in 2006, you had a Sikh Prime Minister, a Muslim President, and a foreign born Western woman at the head of the largest political party in the country. I continued to see widespread and open worship, with young programmers in multinational companies and call centers actively embracing vegetarianism, alcohol and smoke free lives, concern for parents and the elderly, and traditions reflective of their local culture, while seeking the best for India and its future. There was barely a car, rickshaw, work cubicle, or store name that didn't have some reference to spirituality, a picture of a revered deity, a quote from the Koran, or a picture of Jesus.

When I told co-workers in Bangalore that back home in the US you could not openly display religious items like that in the workplace, or even on public buildings, they would look at me, truly bewildered and question……….. Why not? How could someone be offended by the depiction of a saintly person, or a spiritually uplifting phrase? I started to describe our legal structures, constitutional values and lawsuits about co-mingling church and state, and American's love of individualism, but somehow it just didn't make sense to many people in India. They understood the legal aspects, but many were surprised that our society forced people to sweep spirituality under the carpet, at least in public.

Returning to the US, I hung up a simple picture of Gandhi with his beloved Gita (holy book for Hindus) in hand in my office. It has started many interesting conversations, and no one has asked me to remove it.

An Orphanage
in Bangalore

ॐ

A weekend walk around Bangalore was my main diversion, and one that I looked forward to every week. After a work week of contracts, arguments and compliance training, I would find that there was far more entertainment to be had observing Indian city street life than anywhere else. There is a certain freedom that comes from walking in a crowded place with no agenda at all. Within a two block stroll of my apartment, I could see a monkey stealing an apartment dweller's breakfast, or a spontaneous outbreak of male-only dancing to drums in celebration of a religious festival. More frequently, I would be moved to compassion at the sight of hungry person, a leper, or child on the road performing flips and acrobatics at traffic stops in the hopes of getting a few rupees.

One day, I stumbled upon an orphanage run by Mother Teresa's nuns, the Missionaries Sisters of Charity, about 2 miles from my apartment. As a Catholic, in a country where Christians as a whole make up only about 3% of the population, I was always fascinated with the churches and other links to my own religion. Whether it was to simply observe the structure of a church, which would naturally stand out because of the Western style architecture, or an interest in the particular denomination and worship language, I would try to find some connection with other Christians. India has many different Christian rites, including the Malabar Syrian Rite, and various flavors of Anglican denominations, and even some home grown Indian Christian churches. I noted that most Catholics I met came from the west coast of India (Kerala and Goa), and it always fascinated me to wonder how these Catholics got to this place or that. My interest was generally piqued whenever I saw a cross, or statue of the Blessed Virgin. I was also proud as a Catholic to see the universal veneration of Mother Teresa, who did so much for India, and when I peaked over the fence of the orphanage, I could see a picture of Mother Teresa in the hallway, and some of the nuns scurrying about.

Inside the orphanage were abandoned and largely disabled children, most of whom were girls from south India (Karnataka and Tamil Nadu). In India, traditional marriage customs still carry over among the less educated, requiring that fathers pay a "dowry" to the husband's family to complete the marriage arrangements. The dowry could be money or jewelry, or something more practical, like a bicycle, scooter or some livestock if you lived in a village. The tradition, which has been legally "abolished" but does continue in practice, often forces the very poor to talk about the "curse" of having daughters, since multiple daughters can create a crushing financial burden on poor fathers, who see it as their obligation to find husbands for their daughters. When they cannot meet this burden, shame, debt, and occasionally suicide are the result. It is no wonder that to this day a girl born disabled (with little chance of marriage and unable to work) might well be left abandoned, or given up to an orphanage, many of which are run by Christian nuns in India.

I met some of the sisters at the orphanage, dressed in the inspiring white saris with blue trim of Mother Teresa's order. They were happy to meet an interested foreign volunteer. When I asked how I could help out, no one really gave me a task. It was as if they just wanted me to "be" with the children. Given the level of disability of most of the orphans, I felt more comfortable at first acclimating myself to the place by cleaning walls and floors. I could soon see that the nuns were more interested in encouraging interaction with the children, who despite their physical or mental disabilities, were playful like any child, and interested in the stranger in their midst. Over time I came to understand the importance of sitting with the kids, playing with them, talking with them (some were already multi-lingual at age 5!) and helping out with feeding, clean up and keeping a general order to the place. On days that were not too hot, we would take the kids outside in their wheel chairs, stroll around, and sing songs. On several weekends I was joined by other foreign visitors who brought donations and supplies. Many would observe the interaction with the kids from a distance. It is not easy to jump right in and care for the bodily needs of disabled children with limited English.

I was discussing the visits to the orphanage with my neighbor, who lived in my building in Bangalore. She was also working in Bangalore on assignment from Europe, and she was intrigued at the kind of volunteer work I was doing. She revealed to me that as a child her parents went through a difficult time, and after her mother died at a young age, she was placed in a "children's home" in her native country, where she was raised during her early teenage years and into high school. Rather then speaking of this period in her life with regret, she said she understood why her Dad couldn't take care of her and the other kids since he was a single parent without steady income. She told me that her time in the children's home was probably the best thing for her, where adults recognized her intelligence, encouraged her to work hard, and become educated. She also had nutritious food, and was shown love by the older "mother figures" that ran the home.

It wasn't long before my neighbor began to join me at the orphanage, helping out first with the cleaning, and then beginning to feed some of the really disabled children, some of whom couldn't even swallow their food. Over time, her son, an airplane mechanic, came by to help fix up some of the wheel chairs and other broken items in the orphanage during his trips to India. Family and friends visiting me in India often took an interest in both playing with the kids for an afternoon, and financially supporting the work of the Sisters. Almost every trip back to India from the US came with some supplies, some money and prayers for the kids in the orphanage.

I thank God for those aimless walks around India, and for the Spirit's nudging me that first day to go right, instead of left, into the orphanage. To touch another's life, or serve as an unwitting catalyst for change in a person looking to help others, is a great blessing. We really don't know how God acts in our lives, but we should take more walks!

Dr. Bob

ॐ

India, like China and other parts of Asia, still clings to its traditional medical and healing practices while embracing the advances in modern medicines and surgical techniques. The traditional medical practice in India is called "ayurveda," which comes from the Sanskrit "science of life." The main thrust of ayurvedic healing involves balance and equilibrium across the body's many functions. Treatments are entirely natural, and include wide varieties of vegetable and oil based medicines. In India, there are many advanced schools and university level curricula teaching the ayurvedic sciences, and ayurvedic practices (yoga and massage) often complement Western medical practices. Whenever I was occasionally beset by a slight illness during my time in India, a co-worker or friend would always recommend a food or drink that had a "cooling" property, or a fruit with a "warming property," that came from the ayurvedic tradition. For example, yoghurts, despite being heavy, were often suggested to me as a way to "cool" the body down to treat fever. I learned while living in India that food is considered sacred, since it comes from the earth and requires human hands to prepare. We forget this in our fast food society, and few of us these days take the time to actually prepare nourishing meals with fresh ingredients. While we tend to separate food and medicine in the West, Indians and many Asians see food as real nourishment, and capable of healing.

Some of the children in the orphanage run by the Missionary Sisters of Charity routinely required medicines for skin conditions, eyesight problems, or digestive issues. Since I had ready access to a car and driver, and was happy to buy the medicine for the kids, I would often get a list of what was required from the Sisters. The children were regularly visited by a volunteer medical doctor, who would evaluate the children and prescribe the medicines they needed. The sisters themselves, or other visiting ayurvedic practitioners, would also write down certain ayurvedic "prescriptions." It was remarkable to me to observe how one type of illness would receive an ayurvedic treatment, while another would require a "western" medicine. Based on my experience in Bangalore, the ayurvedic stores specialized only in dispensing natural treatments, while other medical "dispensaries" or pharmacies provided the western medicines.

Since I lived near a hospital, I knew that I could easily acquire the western medicines the children needed from the hospital's own internal pharmacy. I had to scramble a bit, however, with the help of a rickshaw driver, to find all the ayurvedic medicines, of which I knew nothing. For one particular potion, I must have traveled 20 kilometers on crowded Bangalore streets (to the delight of my rickshaw driver and his wallet) before I completed the task. I didn't mind it at all. Most of my best times in India were the random strolls or journeys to places unknown. Stopping at a tea stall, trying yet another new and delicious vegetarian dish, or just watching life in this country so different from my own was the best way I knew to fill my free time.

I dropped off the ayurvedic medicines at the orphanage first, and then went home to visit the hospital on the main street where I lived. I had the prescriptions written down and handed them to the hospital pharmacist. I hadn't really thought about the fact that I didn't have a real doctor's prescription, but rather only a handwritten note from the nuns. Of course, in the US, you would never be able to simply request prescribed medicines without a doctor's signature. All I had was Sister's list of the required medicines, in neat handwriting, on a plain scrap of paper. Since the hospital near my apartment was affiliated with a large, prestigious American university medical facility, and likely the rules on dispensing medicine were more strictly enforced, I was politely told that I would need to have a doctor's signature. I tried to explain the situation, that the medicine supply was low at the orphanage, and that the doctor would not be back for a visit until next week. With a large smile and slight shake of the head, the pharmacist told me to try someplace else. I understood and turned around to walk away.

As I was opening the door to leave, the pharmacist called me back. He looked again at the list of medicines, all of which were for relatively minor ailments and in the proper dosages for children. He said, "go down to the end of the block, and go left. Midway down there is a dispensary and they will have the supply." While I was happy to get the recommendation, I asked him "Won't there be a problem since I don't have the doctor's signature? "He smiled again, paused and slightly shook his head as he said, "Just sign your own name at the bottom. They will accept it." I thought about this for a second, and decided "yes," I would simply put my signature at the bottom of the sheet of paper. I realized that a foreigner, dressed in business attire, might be able to pull it off. Sure enough, the other dispensary gave me the medicines the children needed, which I quickly brought over to the orphanage.

Upon delivery to the orphanage, Sister thanked me, and I began to tell her the story. She informed me that when some of their own workers go for the medicines, there is never any issue since they generally go to the same pharmacy, whose attendants have known the nuns for years, and know that the regular doctor prescribes them. I told her that, well, just to speed the process along, I signed the bottom of the paper, so that it looked more like a real prescription and I could get the medicine faster. She looked up at me, and I was a bit hesitant and not sure what her reaction would be. A large smile quickly came across her face, and she said evenly and with conviction, "Oh, That was a very good idea! Now come into the play room and see the children."

The Hero Bicycle

ॐ

One aspect of Indian life that I admire is the collection and reuse of old and used items, most of which would be quickly discarded in the West. Because resources are scarce, most material goods in India are recycled, fixed, saved, collected and re-used. Sitting on my balcony each morning I would hear a man riding through the neighborhood on an old bicycle, ringing a little bell, and shouting "Papers...... paaaaappeeers" as he went up and down the little side streets collecting newspapers. I found his stall one day, with newspapers stacked from floor to ceiling, and I regret not ever stopping in to ask "what do you do with those newspapers?" They were obviously put to some good use, as the collection and storage of the used newspapers was his full time work. I was amazed to find stalls on the side streets where used cellphones were being sold for $10 or less. Parts would be replaced; new keyboards could be obtained for dirty ones, screens replaced. If a cell phone in the US has anything wrong with it, other then the battery, it is more often then not thrown out.... And replaced with a new cell phone! Not in India.......for almost any broken item, there is a replacement part, and a person to repair it.

There was a warm and comforting feeling to all the "oldness" of buildings, cars, scooters and motorcycles around me in Bangalore. Many people still drive "the Ambassador," a rounded and puffy marshmallow- like white car resembling the old checkered cabs in New York City. The cars were manufactured in India, made to last at least 20 years or more, with replacement parts available everywhere. The Ambassador's were simply engineered and could be fixed in almost any village by someone with basic familiarity with cars. These laboring, simply appointed vehicles were heavy, well suited for the subtleties of Indian roads, (and at times the lack of Indian roads), and they were dependable. We rented one for a weekend just to enjoy the trip in this piece of history!

While newer Asian model scooters and motorcycles are found everywhere with familiar names like Honda and Suzuki, Indian roads are still full of vintage scooters called Bajaj Cheetak's....... a joint venture from the early 1950's between Vespa in Italy and a local Indian manufacturer. These are quirky machines, oil would leak out when tipped from one side to another, but their look is classic European from decades ago. While I believe they were still made into the early 90's, their great numbers on the roads today is a testament to their simplicity and ability to be fixed. The "Royal Enfield" motorcycle was yet another throw back to the 1940's and 1950's. Originally a British made cycle, its design was brought to India before the British left, and India is the only place where they are still being manufactured. They look like the old WW I motorcycles, some with gleaming chrome and the Royal Enfield wings on the side. I've heard that the factories which made the Ambassador, Bajaj, and Royal Enfield vehicles rarely, if ever upgraded their tooling, design or introduced new models. It seemed that the old styles worked and so they kept building them the same way. Everyone knows how to fix these vehicles, and so they are economical, and still on the roads of India after decades.

Nowhere is the simplicity of transportation better captured then in the locally made bicycles, the eternal "Hero" cycle, seen everywhere, everyday, every minute on every road in India, in city or village. Hero is the brand name and these bicycles have been made in India for over 70 years to a basic British bicycle design. The Hero cycle is the common transportation experience for all of India. These bicycles clearly look like something out of the 1930's, the type of bike that a postman might use to deliver mail while blowing his whistle, or the bicycle Elmira Gulch rides in the Wizard of Oz after she came to take Toto the dog from Dorothy. Hero bicycles are heavy, made of steel with little attempt over the years to reduce or change the metals to make the bicycle lighter. They are available in 2 colors – black or green.

Until very recently, they had no gears, a simple construction of 2 wheels with metal fenders, a high leather seat, narrow and high handlebars with rudimentary hand brakes, a sturdy spring-loaded carrying trap over the back wheel...... and nothing more. The placement of the handlebars and position of the seats forces you to sit completely upright, straight backed while you peddle, giving riders a casual, pleasant look, as if they were taking a Sunday ride instead of rushing to work. Invariably, some of the bikes would have a seat on the handlebars for a child, with posts added to the front wheel as a foot rest. I would occasionally see a wife sitting side straddle in her sari on the back, sometimes with a baby in her lap. It was truly amazing to watch a small family on a sturdy Hero bicycle getting around the crowded streets of Bangalore.

I nostalgically think back to those still, cool, quiet mornings in Bangalore when I could hear a Hero cycle approach behind me as I walked around before the traffic got heavy. It was not generally the ringing of the heavy old bell on the right hand steering wheel that identified the bicycle, but rather the rhythmic cadence of the chain, just a bit off center, rubbing against the side of the heavy chain guard creating a pleasant and familiar rhythmic scrape in the early morning air. I suppose the rider was happy when his journey took him downhill, as the lack of gears on the older models prevented any real performance driving! The bell, another part of the standard issue Hero cycle that must have come from the first bike bell ever designed, was used constantly to warn the pedestrian that a rider was approaching. This sound is forever etched in my mind. If I close my eyes, I can hear the ringing of this bicycle bell as a drone over all of India for most of the 24 hour long day. I don't think I can ever forget that sound.

Some details of the Hero cycle bear mentioning. Old fashion style hard leather seats, with prehistoric looking springs cushion the Indian bottom on its bumpy journey. These seats are now equipped with a plastic covering, but the old leather seats would get a very shiny, vintage and worn in look over the years. Some people festoon their bicycle with all manner of colorful seat covers, and plastic strings that would fly from the hand grip on the handlebars, adding a touch of style to the old bicycle. My favorite "decoration" was the wrapping of the middle bar connecting the handle bar to the seat post with a colorful placard, often with an advertisers name on it, in English, or Kannada (the local language of Bangalore which looks like the number "8" laying down on its side with squiggles growing out of the circles). These placards might advertise a local store or newspaper. Rather then having a conventional side kick stand, the Hero cycles still come with a spring loaded "stand" which is put into place by swinging the U shaped stand piece under the back wheel, which is then raised off the ground a few inches, and holds the bike in place.

The Hero cycle carries policemen, army men, shop keepers, peddlers, couriers, Everyone! When I decided to get my own, a friend came with me to the shop. I wanted to buy the most basic bicycle I could find. There were many store fronts on Commercial Street selling bicycles, but I went to the one that had the least traffic. The basic bicycle was assembled in front of me in minutes, and with some minor adjustments as to height of the seat, I was quickly off and peddling. The heavy, difficult first couple of turn of the peddles soon transformed into a smooth and steady cadence from which decent speed could be obtained. I had decided on black. No gears and no front seat on the handle bars. In keeping with the Indian tradition of often blessing cars and other vehicles, I got some stickers for the bicycle to cover all my bases, and bring me safety on the crazy and often dangerous Indian roads. Ganesh, the Hindu deity who removes obstacles, is on the back fender, a verse from the Koran is on the middle post, and a picture of Jesus adorns the front fender. My friend, a Hindu, thought it totally appropriate to have multiple religious symbols on a bicycle. Indians would naturally appeal to different incarnations of the deity in Hinduism, and the idea of finding multiple religious traditions in a single place would be entirely natural for Indians, especially when you are praying for safety or good luck.

My friend told me that he still has his father's Hero cycle. It was purchased originally in Mumbai and is 60 years old, rusted, but running smoothly. I'd love to see my grandchildren drive my own Hero cycle!

"The invincible Hero Bicycle"

Banyan Tree Monkey Man

ॐ

For an interesting weekend trip outside of Bangalore, head south on the Mysore Road about 40 kilometers to a small settlement called the Banyan Tree village. As you veer off the highway, you cross over the railroad tracks which connect Bangalore to Mysore, and you always find large numbers of people, most of whom just seem to be "waiting". There is a certain quiet, steady and endearing aspect to these large gatherings of patient, waiting, workers in India. Some people hold bundles, containing coconuts or mangoes waiting to be transported or hawked to passersby. Other people are tethered to some livestock that are carrying goods. Many women are multitasking, as is typical for the Indian woman, carrying produce and babies while older children run around. Most, however, just appear to be waiting for something. Their faces are difficult to read, neither happy, nor particularly anxious. My later model silver Toyota was enough change of scenery to move some of the people out of their thoughts. While cars are ubiquitous in cities and expected on highways, a car filled with Westerners heading towards a small village will attract attention, smiles, waves and sometimes complete, fixated staring. Such cargo doesn't often head out to the Banyon Tree village!

My group of friends from the US wanted a taste of village life without having to go too far from Bangalore. The road going west towards the village morphed from asphalt, to bumpy, broken asphalt, to dirt, crowded with people walking, biking, and scootering in a haphazard stream of movement. I remained forever unable to divine the "rules" of the road in India, regardless of whether I was on a dirt road or a highway. Not only is the left hand lane driving difficult for me conceptually as an American, but I could never reconcile the fact that usually, in the US, the car yields to the pedestrian. In India, it is the complete opposite....... the small vehicle gives way to larger vehicles, and people simply seem to find their hole in the traffic, and run through it.

Drivers lean on their horns to notify people inches away that their vehicle is approaching. While many westerners would have jumped to the left or right at the sound of a blaring horn behind them, with likely a harsh word for the driver, Indian pedestrians gracefully shift the sway of their movement an inch or two to one side without any effort or consternation at the near miss. As if this wasn't interesting enough for my visitors, the road was becoming cratered like the surface of the moon, wearing out the shock absorbers on my car, and bouncing our group every way possible until I asked Harish, my driver, to slow down a bit to avoid impending car sickness on the part of several passengers. Heading further down the road, the stares of the locals became more steady, and people begin to stop in their tracks to observe us.

The bumpy road ended several kilometers further down. On the left towered what looked like a huge football field sized park, with hundreds of high trees, surrounded by a fence. Hardly a sacred spot, or even an unusual destination in a tropical place with vegetation everywhere. But then it hit me....... this wasn't a group of trees or a small forest, it was a single tree, The King of Banyan trees!

Banyan trees are sacred in many Asian cultures, and their reputation in Hindu lore and religious practice as a source of wisdom goes back thousands of years. The "rishis," those who transcribed the sacred Vedic texts from the Gods, are often depicted as meditating under a banyan tree. Wisdom and eternal life are ascribed to the tree since its root structure never seems to end. In fact, the banyan creates a small ecosystem of its own. As the main trunk thrusts upwards yielding to large leafy branches, small off shoots from the branches reach back downwards, find soil, and in time become secondary trunks. The process repeats itself, and over centuries the tree can become a huge, shady, creeping tangle of trunks, branches and paths between them. Almost every village in India has a central banyan tree, often with a cool cement platform built around the base, to provide a shady spot for locals to gather, share stories and serve as a spot for learning or resting.

I had told my visitors, several of which were young boys, about the hundreds of monkeys infesting the banyan tree in this village which I had seen on a previous trip. Monkeys are an ever present source of fun and enjoyment for visitors to India, and their co-existence (usually peaceful!) is respected in parks, gardens, and sometimes balconies. We had arrived around 10am in the morning, and immediately purchased several bags of peanuts from a smiling woman waiting at the gate leading into the banyan cluster. Some enterprising people from the village had made stone paths around the tree, making it easier for visitors to get around, and had put in benches for people to sit and relax, and even a small public toilet. There was now a small entry charge to get into the banyan garden, and a woman selling tickets for 5 rupees (about 10 cents)

The kids ran ahead looking for the monkeys. I'm not sure if it was the time of day, or weather, or season generally, but the many monkeys I observed the last time were just nowhere to be seen. The kids were still in hot pursuit running up and down the trail, but soon resigned themselves to the fact that there was no monkey business around. They started throwing the peanuts at each other to make light of the situation, and the adults sat down on a bench. The beauty of the place was undiminished, but the monkeys would have added a spark for the kids who don't get to see monkeys hanging around in parks in Connecticut.

Soon a local worker came by. He was a portrait of simple, Indian village life. He was wearing a dhoti (the loose fitting skirt favored by rural Indian men) and a haphazard, rolled up cloth turban to keep the heat away (as distinguished from the traditional turban of elegant colors worn by the Sikhs for religious reasons). His face was grizzled with a graying beard, a sympathetic and elegant look, and his skinny legs and bare feet betrayed a man who obviously didn't have much time for relaxing on a sofa or bench.

We said hello, and I asked in broken Hindi/English "Monkeys, kidder hain?" ("Where are the monkeys?"). After a gesture and nod or two, he could tell that the kids were looking for the monkeys as well, and he could see that their bags of monkey food were soon going to waste on the banyan tree floor. He held up his hand in a gesture of "wait", took a few of the peanuts in his hand, and proceeded to quickly hop a fence and walk towards a dense cluster of trees about 100 meters away. We could hear him making calls or whistles, and he soon disappeared into the woods. I really wasn't sure if we would see him again after about 15 minutes of waiting, but since he was kind enough to want to help, I wanted to wait for his return if for no other reason then to thank him for trying.

He soon emerged at a trot, coming out of the cluster, with several large monkeys following him. Smaller monkeys started running towards us as well, and we all jumped up as the kids began to shout "the monkeys are coming!" By this time, some others had come to visit the tree with their young children, and the monkeys, clearly knowing that food awaited them, began climbing the fence and perching on branches, as they surveyed which children held the bags of food. The kids' initially timid gesture of throwing some nuts at the monkeys soon became a monkey-child pas de deux, as both creatures more comfortably approached each other to wild shouts of glee from the visitors. Food was being placed in the monkeys eager hands, and the kids were asking to purchase more food. The initial stream of brown mustard colored monkeys being lead by our monkey finder friend soon turned into a huge pack of people and animals. Cameras were snapping, and brazen monkeys were reaching into the bags themselves for peanuts. The kids were laughing and scrambling behind parents when the monkeys got too close for comfort. This event would be the highlight of the trip that day and the faces of the kids, both local and foreign held smiles as broad as the banyan tree itself.

I saw the old man leaning against the fence, a contented smile on his face, just watching the action and taking a few minutes rest. I approached him, and tried to tell him how happy he made the kids, and how great it was that he went to this trouble for us. I asked to take a picture with him, and without making a big deal, I tipped him. He had brought the place to life, and created a memory for those children that is strong to this day. I thought for a moment of the blessing it is to take a little time for others, and how a positive gesture witnessed by youngsters can leave an indelible and lifelong impression.

When my son and his friends get together, they still talk about "that monkey man dude at the banyan tree." In the eyes of those children, this village man became a superhero. He could have done no greater deed then to summon the monkeys!

The Tailor

ॐ

For many of us there is still a real charm and appeal to handmade goods, specifically when made for the purchaser at his or her request. In the West, there are so few opportunities to actually purchase something completely unique, or perfectly fitted, or simply made by hand. In India, most things are still made by hand. Machines are expensive, and few other then the wealthiest companies can afford heavy equipment. In India labor is cheap, people need work, and they use their hands to get it done.

Within a stone's throw of my apartment I watched a hotel being built over a two year period. A hundred women would carry dirt on their heads out of an excavated foundation for months. A back hoe or dump truck would have done the job in a week or less. The foundation was mixed by hand by men who shoveled sand and broken rock into a large container with water, turned this tumbler around, and soon created cinder block for the hotel, right on the same spot. Metal posts to harden the foundation were brought in by a truck and then "cut" to size by two men, one of whom would position the metal rod on a small fulcrum, while the other would bend the pole back and forth until it snapped. As the building rose, there was no elevator or elaborate metal scaffolding in place. Instead, hundreds of large pieces of bamboo were lashed together with cord, which allowed barefoot construction workers to climb up to the next floor being worked on. Since many of the people came from villages outside of Bangalore, most workers lived on the site, cooking, cleaning and sleeping under the previously finished floor, which now served as a roof. Children were running everywhere. I always prayed that one of them wouldn't get hurt in the activity. It was fascinating to watch, however, and I suppose I got the same amount of stares back at me if I stood looking too long.

Further down the road, in the market area, I passed a series of tailors. In India, somewhat in defiance of normal competitive commercial practices, tradesmen tend to join together, their shops being located next to each other instead of spread out in the "normal" or western way to reduce competition among rivals and achieve a "prime" location. I learned that this practice was actually more beneficial to the tailors in a particular area. Indeed, often times they might have come originally from the same place, or they might be related in some way, and as such they were motivated to help each other out as needed to protect their own rights and interests. I wondered why so many were named "Rao"... and I learned that this particular bunch of tailors were all related, and had come from Maharasthra, the state in which Mumbai/Bombay is located.

One thing you quickly learn about living in India is the need for cool, airy, and loose fitting clothing. Women favor the sari or salwar chameez because it allows for movement, and helps one stay cool. For men, the traditional skirt/dhoti, or "pajama" (loose fitting thin pants) served the same purpose, although they are not generally worn any more to an office environment. As for shirts, most men had some kind of colorful, plaid shirt, always worn outside of the pants, rarely tucked in. I saw this both for laborers and office workers. Of course, it was much cooler to leave the shirt out. Such shirts were tailored in a different way, squared off at the bottom, and shortened a bit so as to not hang down too far. None of my factory made shirts were cut this way and to wear them untucked, while comfortable, looked silly, for they were cut longer in the front and back, and hung down much further then necessary. I decided I would get the Rao's to make me a shirt. !!

I recall the first time walking into this small storefront on Dispensary Road near Commercial Street in Bangalore. There was a balding man with a mustache arranging cloth, and his brother, neatly dressed and working behind the large work desk. There were several pictures and statutes of Ganesh, complete with blinking lights and incense burning near the door which opened to the street. Large rolls of beautiful cloth, for shirts, pants, and suits, were neatly folded and lined up sardine style against the wall, to be examined upon request. There was a picture of a man dressed in a kurta pajama and turban, the traditional "genie" look, which I soon learned was the man who started the store in Bangalore 60 years ago. The shop was now being proudly run by his sons, the two Rao brothers.

The Rao brothers were exceedingly polite, spoke beautiful English, and enjoyed asking me about my doings and wandering in India. They even expressed surprise at my few Hindi words, and took a lot of time to carefully measure me when I told them what I was looking for. "How did I want the cut of the shirt, did I want buttons on the collar? Did I want a loose or fitted shirt? Did I want some tea? Now, let's look at the cloth itself. Did I need a business shirt or a short sleeve shirt for weekends? Both? "I loved the beautiful, casual cloths, and colorful blue and yellow plaids and madras styles. I kept thinking of seeing this kind of material in the "hiqh quality" US retail catalogs. I knew that those shirts clearly came from factories, but must have been inspired by the raw material I saw here in India. Some materials were like silk, others pure cotton. The colors were dazzling, and it was truly difficult to decide what to order. I decided to go with one work shirt (I had plenty of them already) and several short sleeve casual shirts as a first try.

A ticket was written up very formally. I remember that printed sheet of paper, with the Rao name elegantly engraved on each page, and my personal dimensions neatly written on the ticket. Pieces of the chosen cloth were cut off and stapled to the ticket, and a small deposit was made to cover the cost of the material which would be cut to size from the large roll of cloth. I was told to return in three days.

I could hardly wait! I came back with my ticket in hand, and was greeted by one of the brothers who was at the work desk. It struck me how content these two seemed to be in this small work place day after day, for so many years. He was very carefully pinning a piece of elegant material for a handmade suit. I noticed his dedication, his look of peaceful serenity as if he was always meant to be a tailor, and making clothing was simply an extension of his being. Maybe that is what happens when people accept the trade of the family as a given. "We are tailors." There is no angst over "what will I be when I grow up?" as we have in the West; rather, for these men, they simply will do the work of their fathers, and make an honest living with their hands.

There was some quiet chanting coming from an old radio in the corner which gave the place a sacred feeling as night began to fall in Bangalore.

He told me that his brother had just gone to another shop to find a button for one of my shirts. It was a blue button and they had run out of that appropriate size for the collars. It would be no problem for him to find such a button from one of the neighboring shops, and he soon came back with a hearty greeting. The returning brother went to the back room, and soon emerged with my four shirts neatly folded, with some tissue paper separating them, and with a copy of the ticket fastened to the top. Without thinking, I asked to try one on. This surprised the two of them, who must have known that there was no question that the shirts were perfectly made for me. I then noticed that there was no changing room in the little shop. They invited me to change in the backroom. Of course the shirt was perfect.

The amount paid for the four shirts was less then the price of a single shirt purchased from a US retail store. Holding these shirts in my hand, I thought about how I picked out the cloth, it was cut and stitched for me by skilled craftsman, whom I got to know personally, and who worked in my neighborhood. I felt a strange connection to "old days" when commerce was not global, or even regional, but based on the village. The shirt felt good next to my skin, like a glove. I brought every one who came to visit me to those tailors over a two year period, and would frequently stop in to chat with the brothers whenever I was in the area.

Those shirts hang in my closet with the label "Rao Tailors," Dispensary Road, Bangalore, stitched inside each collar. They are among my greatest souvenirs from my time in Bangalore.

Blessed are those who are happy in their work! Their customers will be pleased, their product will be of highest quality, Ganesh will remove all their obstacles, and they will be content with enough.

Life near the Jungle

ॐ

It is amazing to think that there are still places where tigers roam freely, and where people can still come into direct conflict with them. I have read that in India several hundred people a year are killed by tigers, generally in the Bengal region of Calcutta, where villages expand, farmers extend their cultivation into jungle regions, and the inevitable encroachment results in death – usually of the farmer. Similarly, elephant herds have destroyed huts and farms for the same reason in more remote areas, and crocodiles, called "muggers," will often lie in wait below the surface of the river while women and children wash clothing or bathe. Between battling these animals, (did I mention the ubiquitous cobras?) the highly destructive monsoons, and the general scarcity of resources in much of the country, life in India is challenging, and can be dangerous at times to say the least.

In planning a trip for some visiting friends, I found out that we could go into the jungle regions of India and see some of this wildlife in its natural state. One area in particular is called the Kabini jungle, located about 300 km south of Bangalore. The site has a relatively well furnished lodge area and guesthouse set up to host visitors for weekend trips. In the jungle, you get the chance to see elephants, wild buffalo, peacocks, and, if you are lucky, tigers! Due to the presence of experienced guides and naturalists, who know the area well and take tourists around by jeep, I felt safe enough to book the trip with family and friends. After living in the city for a year, I was ready to set out one weekend to learn more about India's wildlife.

The tour was fantastic. After an introductory session with the local naturalists and lunch, we set out for an evening jeep ride into the deeper jungle to spot wildlife. Tigers tend to be solitary, come out at night to hunt, and are in general reclusive. They hide during the day and rest somewhere cool, away from the jeep paths and the sound of the engines. In a light rain, it didn't take long before our guide, who was in radio contact with a spotter down the road, found a herd of elephants grazing by a pond. We approached carefully, and got within 50 feet of one of the largest wild elephant herds in Southeast Asia. From heavily tusked elephants clearing their way down to the water to small young ones seeking the shelter of a mother's shoulders or tail, we watched at least 80 wild elephants watering down as the day yielded to night against a blue and orange sky. It was a time of great, almost primordial silence, and we all knew that we were witnessing something that few have the opportunity to ever see. I felt a stronger connection to the deeper, wild state of nature which we in cities and suburbs have lost. Over the next few days we saw buffalo, and other huge horned animals, like the gower, quietly grazing. Monkeys were everywhere, and we saw more elephants, wild peacocks and wild pigs. We were shown fresh tiger tracks, evidence that tigers were in the area, but alas, the tigers did not reveal themselves to us on that trip.

One afternoon during a mid-day break, my friend Gerry and I decided to walk out of the compound into the village a bit. We walked a mile down the road, made a right hand turn to a rice paddy farm, and took the same path that locals were using in their day to day farming to get to the fields. About a quarter mile off the road, we watched several workers bent over in the rice paddy field, plucking or planting, some ankle deep in water, some clearing with machete-like implements. Again, I felt the same primordial, ancient stillness of the dawn of agricultural life surround me. Not a single machine-made sound could be heard, and in surveying the area, it struck me that everything I could see was completely natural. Only people, animals, land, water. No electric wire, no telephone pole, not a car or truck. The scene was tranquil, peaceful, and could have been from the 1800's, the 1500's, 1200's - or from the Garden itself.

As we approached one field to get a look at the kind of work people were doing, I could see the few workers there stop and simply stare. Gerry is about 6 foot 3, blond, and stood out against the background like some foreign giant in sneakers, baseball cap, and a tee shirt. For many villagers in rural India who have never seen a tall, oddly dressed foreigner, let alone in THEIR village, the experience was likely as surreal for them as it was for us. I'm sure in their minds the questions arose, who are these people, why are they here? ...... but the guileless stare, emotionless and genuine of these few workers made me smile. We were deep in Kannada country, the ancient and local language of Karnataka, previously the Kingdom of Mysore. My few words of Hindi didn't go very far, and English was more or less out of the question.

The light mist which accompanied us in the jungle had turned into a torrential rain in a span of 30 seconds. We were far from the jungle lodge, and quite a bit from the main road to get us back to the lodge. The workers, all in dhotis and barefoot, signaled us to follow them. At the edge of a clearing we saw a one room hut made of wood and cement that the farmers were running towards. I wasn't sure if the rain itself prevented the farm work from continuing, or if there was a fear of lightning, or if this was simply a convenient time for a break.

We were soon invited into this hut, which seemed to be strewn with farm implements, some cots, clothing, some teapots and a single light bulb hanging from the ceiling, which didn't work. There wasn't much talk at all inside for a few minutes as we were all huddled together against the outside rain. We just sort of looked at each other, with the occasional smile. My "namaste" with hands together greeting was returned. A manager of some sort then came into the hut, perhaps having heard himself that some foreigners were poking around in the fields. He could speak a bit of Hindi, and I told him we were visiting Kabini, the jungle lodge. He said "accha," – "I see," and had a friendly way about him. When the rain stopped, we said our thanks, "dohnewad", and left the hut to get back to the road. Turning around to look behind me, these farmers were still staring at us, although their posture seemed a bit more relaxed.

One of them still had a big smile on his face. I turned and waved to him. He waved back, still staring at us, and I could see the gentle head nod by which many Indians communicate positive energy, and contentment.

I realized we had both just glimpsed something completely new in our lives. And there was a connection. There would be stories told to family and friends of the strange encounter on both sides later that day.

Sometimes such encounters only happen when you get off the main road, and when you are willing to get wet!

The Jain Statue

ॐ

The largest monolithic statue in the world, carved from a single piece of stone, is located near the city of Hassan about a 5 hour drive from Bangalore. It is a 60-foot tall depiction of Bahubali, one of the saints of the Jain religion. In the statue, Bahubali stands upright, completely naked, with an expression of incredible calm, serenity and peacefulness. The statue was built about 1000 years ago, and is on top of a hill requiring a climb of hundreds of steps just to get to the base of the statue. The base of the statue holds some of the oldest inscriptions in Kannada and Tamil, two important languages of southern India. The place is called Shravanabelagola and is an extremely important pilgrimage site for Jains. Jainism is an ancient religion in India which mandates a strict code of non-violence for all living things. The statue of Bahubali is remarkable, an incredible engineering feat, and from its top offers an amazing and breezy view of the Hassan district of Karnataka.

Whenever I see these amazing, almost bombastic expressions of religion, and the tolerance of the people in India to accept faith in God as something natural and good, I think of how in the US religious expression is at times suppressed. Few outward signs among Americans would ever reveal ones religion, or any religion for that matter. We rarely take the time in public to thank God for our food or offer a blessing publicly at work. In fact, many Americans feel uncomfortable talking about religion, their faith, and what they believe in. Someone who speaks of religion or faith might be called a "holy roller", an arch conservative, a fanatic. Our churches are often ornate, and in some towns they can even be the tallest building around. But in America, religion is often relegated to a few hours a week inside the church or temple itself, with few outward expressions of worship or devotion. I wonder if we would be a better society if we all felt more comfortable with religious symbols on the streets, at work, or wherever. I would be happy to see the Crescent of Islam, a cross, the Star of David, and other symbols of God coexisting on our streets or at work.

Thankfully, this is the case in India! Religious festivals are the most colorful, noisy, lavish, extended and happy gatherings of all. Cooking, dancing, music and singing explode onto the streets at these religious festivals, and thousands or worshippers attend them. Almost every day, in some village in India, a religious festival is being celebrated. Every time a worker failed to show up at my flat, or an appointment was missed, it was invariably blamed on "a festival." For my driver, his yearly village festival was so important that I would give him several days off to attend it and enjoy it with his family.

Even during the work week, there would be "mini" festivals in Bangalore celebrated by different communities of people who were commemorating their particular deity or local belief from their village. I fondly remember sitting on my balcony in Bangalore and hearing the rhythmic beat of a drum in the distance, or a communal song indicative of some devotion somewhere in the city. It would often draw me outside to see what was going on. These festivals, the Muslim call to prayer, and the ringing of the bells from my local church reminded me that in India, people are really comfortable with the Divine in their day to day lives.

One day we decided to take the long drive out to Shravanbelagola. We figured we would see the statue itself, and then head over to a close by city to see some old "Hoysala" stone temples that were also about 900 years old. When we arrived in Hassan, near the Jain statue, we were shocked. The place was absolutely packed with pilgrims, and we could barely get to the gate to remove our shoes before ascending the steps. People of all ages and sizes were going up and down the steep stone stairs to get to the statue. Some were even being carried up by porters who were on hand to help the elderly, or the infirm. Literally, those people were placed on a cot, and for an offering, they would be carried up the hundreds of stone steps to the foot of the statue! We didn't know it, but the Spirit had helped us decide to visit Shravanabegola during the very week of the most important festival for Jains in the area – the Mahamastakbheshika, which occurs once every TWELVE years! The next such devotional festival will be in 2018.

We joined the crowds and headed up the steps, stopping to sip water, and to take a look at the view. People were crowding past us, up and down, and the atmosphere was lively, happy, and lighthearted. Some people coming down the stairs appeared to have red and yellow paint on them, with encrusted flower pedals in their hair and clothing. We soon found out why. A huge scaffold had been built next to the statue of Bahubali allowing pilgrims to stand on a platform just above the head of the statue. From the platform they were pouring coconut milk, colored ghee (oil), sandalwood (a scented wood considered sacred in India) and all manner of colored powders and offerings which were streaming down the face of the 60 foot high statue. Old Bahubali would start out red, and then turn white and pink, then yellow as the various colors and oils mixed and co-mingled over his body down to his feet. A band was playing some happy music, and people were lined up by the hundreds to make the climb up to the head of Bahubali and throw flowers, sing and say prayers over the statue. We observed this amazing scene in wonder. Never had I seen such joy in any religious group. We were about 1000 feet in the air, next to one of the largest statues in the world, among people in pure and welcoming celebration at this religious festival.

What was it all about? Jainism embraces non-violence in the extreme. The belief in the utter sacredness of all life compels observant Jains to only eat vegetables that grow above the ground or come from trees, as if the notion of breaking open the earth to gather vegetables was a violation. Bread making is also done according to strict guidelines for the harvesting of grains, and the length of time that the flour may be stored before use. As in Hindu belief, the idea of self surrender, control over ones desires through renunciation, meditation and fasting unite Jains with so many Asian contemplative faiths.

According to Jain religious history, Lord Bahubali was forced to fight his brother to retain his Kingdom centuries ago. Instead, he chose to renounce his Kingdom rather then do harm to his brother, and as such he is worshipped as the perfect example of purity in conquering anger, jealousy, pride and self centeredness. His face as captured in the stone is reminiscent of his frequent and deep meditations. He is in a state of bliss, peace and tranquility–so much so that vines appear to be creeping up his body! His naked form is intended to convey the complete renunciation of everything in his life but God. It is amazing to me how many religions reinforce this concept of self sacrifice, self control and renunciation to "clear the path" for God in our lives.

At the foot of Lord Bahubali pilgrims were touching his feet, soaking in the oils and brightly colored milks being poured from above in giddy prayer. Priests were spread face down at the base of the statue, and all around the monolith people were praying, flinging flowers and enjoying this once in a 12-year spectacle. A woman came up to my red headed son Nicholas, who was 10 at the time, and hugged him, touching his hair and face and remarking how great it was that we were there to celebrate with them. Of course, we had no idea that this weekend would be basically the once in a lifetime chance to witness the Mahamastakbheshika.

Just then, down at the base of the statue, walked an old man, completely naked, who was bathing himself in the colorful liquids streaming off of Lord Bahubali's body. He was completely oblivious to everything around him, and like the statue itself, was a portrait of silent prayer and worship. Soon I saw people coming up to him, bowing before him, touching his feet, although many averted their eyes from his nakedness. He was a saddhu, an extreme holy man who lives by the alms of others, has freed himself of worldly concerns, and clothes himself only with what God has given him. These saddhus have no concern for what happens outside in the world. For the saddhus, who still number in the hundreds of thousands in India, the interior life is what matters, finding the Soul wherin God dwells in each of us. In India such a man is often held in higher esteem than a political dignitary, or a movie star. There is great respect for holiness, and holy people, in India.

I'm sure such a man would be immediately arrested in most parts of the West as a lunatic, or rabble rouser. In India, people stand in awe of his simplicity, and seek his blessing.

The statue of Bahubali is decorated with offerings during the Jain Festival

Harish the Driver

ॐ

Traffic in Indian cities can try one's patience.

I don't mean the occasional rush hour delay that might slow down one's ride to work. I mean traffic that is so terrible that one debates whether it is better to get out of the car, and walk to work instead of driving! My 9 kilometer (about 5.5 miles) drive to the office could take 20 minutes if done in the middle of the night or early morning, an hour if done at 8am, or two hours if there was the slightest disturbance, accident, or visiting dignitary tying up the roads. Bangalore was never designed to handle the 6- plus million people clogging the roads daily.

I was always amused at the "visiting dignitary" delays while living in Bangalore. First off, the newspaper would publish, in advance, that there would be road closings at certain times of the day. The effected roads would be listed, with accurate, but typically annoying road closure times that lasted for hours. Next, on MG Road in the center of town, a huge, colorful and generally pretty floral welcome sign would alert people as to "who" was coming to town. While some names were generally recognizable, eg., Sonia

Gandhi, Head of the Congress Party, others seemed to stretch a bit to assure true VIP treatment was meted out, consistent with the guidelines of protocol and hierarchy. I recall one time seeing "Bangalore Welcomes His Excellency, Javier Rodrigues, the Deputy UnderSecretary for Commerce from Venezuela!!" (name changed, since I cannot remember the real name!). Imagine the pride you would feel upon passing this handmade sign with your name as large as life in floral splendor. After picking up the dignitary at the airport, tons of police would line up in full uniform with radios every 200 meters, relaying signals to each other. "He's coming, yes, the car is in view now, stand back, VIP approaching."

At times there was a certain archaic formality to the whole event, one which harkens back to the days of the British Raj. Just as often, I was reminded of the Monty Python brass band, the certain foolish absurdity to these displays, which were complete with full regal pomp and circumstance. On a serious note, the whole process reflects India's respect for hierarchy and welcoming attitude towards visitors, something which made my time there so fascinating and warm. It is also a reflection of the vestiges of British regal proceedings which seemed to have invaded the Indian establishment's DNA, even after over 60 years of independence. Nothing of importance can happen without a big ceremony, parade, puja, and the shutting down of roads. While an interesting spectacle, it was nonetheless very, very frustrating to be caught in a road closing when you really needed to get somewhere fast.

So...... thus comes the need for a driver. My employer pretty much insisted that we hire drivers, instead of driving ourselves, because of the traffic, the road conditions, and the strong likelihood of accidents arising from the chaos on the streets. Someone not familiar with the situation was much more likely to get in trouble then a local. I simply had to spend too much time in my car, and although I never enjoyed reading in the back seat, or working on my laptop, it was much less frustrating then driving! Finally, and perhaps most importantly, all of the above were infinitely more complicated by the fact that India adopts the British system of driving on the left hand side of the road, with the steering wheel on the opposite side of the car. While I have ventured to drive in such a manner on the quiet roads of the Irish countryside, doing so in India would have been both a futile and fatal experience!

I had fired my first driver, who I hired largely because he was a Christian, and he had tried to convince me that it was harder for him to get a job, as a minority, then for a Hindu. Religion coming into employment again! He had asked me early on to help him pay for his daughter's Catholic school fees, which I did because I though it worthwhile for the daughters to have a better education then could be obtained at the ill funded municipal schools. I believe that the advancement of young women through education in India is the key to India realizing its true potential. Finally, I thought that my gesture would increase his loyalty and dedication to the job, since I occasionally needed him on call after hours and on weekends. While things worked out initially, multiple episodes of tardiness, expired licenses, several traffic tickets, and finally catching him driving his friends around in my car while I was at work, forced our employment relationship to come to an end. I gave him a month's pay, told him that he owed me nothing for his daughter's education, and took the keys. It took me awhile to find another driver, having been scared off by the first one, and my mind darted back and forth between getting a scooter (fun, but dangerous) and taking rickshaws (also fun, but not always reliable!)

Finally, Harish showed up as my driver... a portrait of stability, respect and dependability. He came from a local village outside of Bangalore, and had been driving for my neighbor, for about 2 years in the city. For awhile we shared his services since our work locations were more or less in the same direction. I hired him full time when my neighbor's assignment to India ended, and I was eager to pay him higher then market wage before someone else snatched him up. When so much of your time, and therefore your emotional health, is dependent on your driver, your investment priorities shift!

For an American, having "help," whether a maid, driver or cook in the house, is often seen as an invasion of privacy, even a loss of independence. While Indians with some money, and many Europeans and South Americans view having servants as normal and proper, Americans generally want to do things for themselves, and have a difficult, if not altogether suspicious view of personal assistants, like drivers. Can I trust him to put gas in the car, to give me the correct change, to drive my family and friends around? Would he drive my car back to my garage after he dropped me off at the airport, or would he drive his friends around for the week I was away on travel? In India today, infrastructure challenges, traffic, and the fact that many women now work outside the home make these kinds of hired workers necessities, once the bond of trust is established.

Harish was cheerful, with an easy, boyish smile. As the first face one would see in the morning on the way to work, this meant a lot! The only vice I could ever detect in him was a self proclaimed enjoyment of food. Although he was a vegetarian, he had a slight plumpness which added to his youthful appearance. He was an observant Hindu, mild mannered, and I never saw him drink, smoke, eat meat, or act in a disrespectful manner in anyway. He was always prompt, and looked upon his work, his duty or "dharma," with pride. He was quick to assist passengers with car doors, take bags and place them in the vehicle, and did so in a way that never made anyone feel uncomfortable. In particular, when my neighbor was working late at her office, he would insist on waiting in the parking lot for her after hours just in case something might happen. There had been several attacks on women during the third shift at the call centers in Bangalore, and he saw safety and protection as his role as well. On longer trips when we would stop for food, I would eat lunch with Harish, and thus began to learn a little more about his life, family, and aspirations. Some Indians saw eating with their driver as crossing a line, since discipline would be more difficult if relations became familiar. I wouldn't know, because I never had the occasion to discipline him.

His village was about 30 miles from Bangalore and was located on a beautiful river and lake that was formed by a water treatment operation set up by the British in the 1920's. Harish's father, and grandfather were workers at the plant, and a "colony" grew up around this location for the workers which included a school, temple, row houses, and lots of open space. There was a lovely old British bungalow "guest house" which could be used for events by the locals. As a municipal or government employee, the small apartment in the colony was likely heavily subsidized as a perk for Harish' father, and his parents, grandmother, and several unmarried siblings lived in a 2 or 3 room one story row apartment, no bigger then the size of a garage. About 10 such dwellings, made of cement, were connected, facing another row of ten. These housed the workers and their families. The stability of the work, and relative low cost of village living enabled Harish' family to live with some meager comforts - at least without the big city's frustrations.

For a while Harish had wanted my neighbor, her son, and me to visit his village. I felt a bit strange at the request, since most of the Indians I had consulted told me that it really wasn't a good idea to get "too close' with the people you employed as hired helpers. Mostly, the concern expressed to me by locals was that you could wind up becoming a "bank" for all their monetary needs, since their circumstances were generally difficult. This, in fact, had been my experience with the first driver, whose endless requests for advances meant that his average end of the month take home pay was a small remaining percentage of the agreed to salary. I was overcome, however, with the notion of visiting the place which Harish talked of constantly. He told us about the fresh fish they would catch, and the food his mom and sisters would prepare. He told us about the temple in the middle of the river, and the sunsets. His mom had even embroidered a shirt for me in the local Kannada language (I think it is my name phonetically spelled, with the date and the city name "Bangaluru!"). One Saturday morning, we decided to go out to visit Harish' village.

What a peaceful place! You could see for miles from the guesthouse, out on to fields, the lake, the grazing cows. The guesthouse itself was simple, white stone work, very colonial, British-looking, and had a veranda with fans to cool the patio down. Monkeys were frequent visitors to the patio, especially when there was food around. These days not many people stayed at the guest house, so foreign visitors were a pretty big deal.

Harish had told his extended family about our visit, and there were about 25 people there to greet us. The steps to the family's small home had been adorned with Hindu symbols for good luck. Despite the very small rooms, we were all given seats, had fresh lime soda and some chips, and made pleasant, albeit highly translated and choppy conversation! I still remember the modest paintings and statues of Ganesh all over the place. Harish' Grandmother, in a tan sari with long, braided white hair, sat next to me. She was quite old, and elegantly adorned with earings and nose rings and bangles. There was such a dignity to this woman, who had lost her husband years before. She was content with her life and her purpose or station in life, and her face radiated the kind of serenity that one achieves when they faithfully turn the wheel of life, according to their duty.

We walked around the grounds, saw the marvelous engineering work which took water from the river, cleaned it, and pumped it out to the lake. In turn, this lake then became a fresh water reservoir for the city of Bangalore. The temple in the middle was only accessible by boat. Hawks and eagles soared around everywhere. Large rocks lay on the shore of the lake and Harish' nieces and nephews played on the rocks. You forget when you live in a noisy city how nice the countryside can be. I still remember the quiet, the gentle lapping of the water on the shore, the huge birds flying lazily on the summer breeze. It was the stillness of nature; everything seemed in balance and alignment. Nature was worshipping God.

When we got back to the guesthouse, everyone was there and there were large buckets of rice and chappati (bread) and banana leaves being spread out on the table in south Indian style. As if the vegetable dishes weren't delicious enough, chicken and fish had been prepared for us, kebab style. The women didn't eat with us, but served the food and helped with drinks. I was a little conscious that this was quite an expense for Harish, and I wanted to leave plenty of food as leftovers for these children. But they would not hear of us passing on seconds. When we finished, the women quickly took their meal in the next room on the floor while we were invited to lay down in the guestrooms, nap, or just sit on the verandah. We soon re-assembled at the guesthouse and began to sing, play some instruments, and chat. The kids began to dance, mimicking some bollywood moves, and although generally very shy, they warmed up enough. I was being called "uncle" in no time.

We made at least three such visits to Harish's village. His home is etched in my memory as a place of decency, tranquility, hard work, and nature's beauty. The village life was better then the city life, and I now know why Harish would try to drive his motorcycle out there every time he could. On the last visit, I met the girl he would marry. She was his cousin, a bright and attractive young girl of about 16 years old. Although invited to the wedding, I had already returned to the US when Harish and Lakshmi got married, and could not make the trip – although I wanted to.

When I left India, I gave almost everything that I wasn't bringing back to the US to Harish and the orphanage where I volunteered. I knew that Harish' family could use blankets, sheets, and kitchenware, and I hoped that they would find a use for some other small appliances, or sell them. Their gesture of friendliness and openness at the village touched me deeply, and still does. I think of the village often, and hope that things are still the way I remember them. I gave Harish an early wedding present before I left.

So turns the wheel of life, the dharma chakra. Somehow that village gave me a glimpse of the way the Lord wants us to live. Be grateful to have enough, take care of your surroundings, do your work with dignity, enjoy some down time with your family and friends, rest when you can. Be at peace with nature.

My Daughter
wants to Marry You!!!

ॐ

I was always the only foreigner at the little Carmelite Chapel near my apartment, except when I brought foreign visitors.

The chapel and its attached nun's residence was not a real parish, and therefore had no regular priest or school attached to it. In addition, it was situated in a quiet, pretty and predominantly Muslim section of Bangalore, on Ali Askar Road, near my own flat, and behind a large fence and lush rain trees. The chapel was hard to see, easily missed, and thus did not attract many people to its somewhat hidden doors. Often daily mass was said only for the cloistered nuns themselves, or perhaps several locals familiar with the place who lived within easy walking distance. I would sit near the back of the ten-row chapel simply taking in the style of dress, the subtle differences in worship style, and trying to figure out how Roman Catholics found there way to this little chapel.

One day I saw my friend's maid, Bebita, attend local mass. She was working for a lovely Hindu family in the area, and we arranged for her to cook me several meals each week. I didn't know that she was Christian. Since she cooked my meals in the home of my friends, which is where she lived, I never really met her out of the house, and didn't see her often at all. When I finally figured out that she was attending mass at the same church, at the encouragement of her employers, I spent some time talking to her one day after mass.

Her English was pretty good, and the family that she was working for apparently had a somewhat parental role in her life, as she was far from her native village. In fact, they were actually trying to find her a marriage proposal! This was the first time I realized that even Christians in India might go through arranged marriages, more or less. When it came to things like marriage traditions, the predominant culture of India would often cross religious lines, and a common "Indian-ness" would win out over religious differences. I say this because in general, few Christian marriages are arranged in most Western societies. But in India, the notion of dating before marriage is not really encouraged. Thus spouses are often "found," even in Muslim and Christian circles. In Bebita's case, arranging a marriage was likely more comfortable for her particular circumstance, since the family for whom she worked was Hindu, where marriages are still commonly arranged among most of the population.

Bebita told me that she had seen me at church several times. When I said "Really? why didn't you say hello?" I realized that her shyness, and perhaps even her own view of her place in the world, or mine, prevented her from wanting to reach out to me. I walked part of the way home with her one day after mass, and we talked comfortably. I could tell, however, that when we passed other people on the street, she would get quiet and look down. I guess it is not hard to imagine that a local maid walking and talking on the street with a foreigner is uncommon, and maybe even uncomfortable.

One day after Mass I was talking to Sister Raphael, the superior of the Carmelites, just outside the Chapel. I noticed a woman around my own age dressed in a beautiful sari, and a girl that I took to be her daughter, perhaps around 18, equally beautifully dressed. They seemed to be looking at me in the courtyard, just quietly whispering. In fact, I was a bit distracted by these women as I spoke with Sister, who eventually said goodbye and then efficiently went about her business of locking up the chapel. In a cloistered convent, the young nuns are really full time residents of the convent itself, devoting their lives mostly to prayer. Gates and doors are shut when public prayer is not in session.

I walked over to the mother and daughter, who were clearly waiting to talk to me.

The older woman started asking me the same standard questions that most locals ask foreigners, if they are bold enough. "Where are you from?" she said, in excellent English. "America," I answered. "What is your work here?" I told her that I was a lawyer, working here in town. "How long will you stay here?" I told her about two years. The questions were a bit invasive, but nevertheless I answered them, since I enjoyed meeting new people, I myself was new to the country, and this was the church courtyard. "Where is your family?" I told her that I didn't have any family actually living here in Bangalore. Before I could begin the explanation of my corporate assignment, my travels back and forth, and how my family was staying in the US, a smile came on the woman's face, and she brightened up completely. "You are a Catholic?" I said that I was.

"My daughter would like to marry a foreigner," she said. "It is not so good here for a good Christian girl, and I would like her to go abroad. So you are not married? My daughter would be a good wife for you. You need an Indian wife." I was stunned. The girl herself, who was attractive, but shy, hadn't even looked up at me during her mother's interrogation. She looked down at the ground; I suppose waiting for what I would say. The fact that I had to be almost 25 years older then the girl didn't seem to matter much, nor the fact that I didn't know these people, their family, or the girl herself. I said "Ummm, well, that is very nice, thank you so much. I am married, my family stays in America, they will be here for Easter and you can meet them at church."

The woman was a bit crestfallen, but recovered nonetheless, with additional questions. "Do you have any brothers or friends who might want to marry my daughter? I would really like to get her out of India. She should go abroad. I would like her to marry an Italian, do you know any? "I really started to laugh at this exchange. I couldn't figure out if "Italian" was a good nationality because of the location of the Vatican and the Pope, or perhaps, it was because Sonia Gandhi, an Italian born woman of high political influence in India, had paved the way for Italians in India? I told her jokingly that I would see what I could do. I was part Italian anyway, by background!

My driver was waiting for me and I had to get to work. I said "see you at church next time!" and got into my car. The image of this mother and beautiful daughter, at 7:30am, on a weekday, dressed in colorful sari's, standing outside church, and seeking me out for marriage was a lot to handle for the 45 minutes drive to the office. It gave me some things to think about for quite sometime. I was particularly impressed by the mother's spirit, exploring every angle to get what she believed to be the best for her daughter.

I hope that this girl gets the chance in life for more than a worthy husband. Education will ensure that her skills and ambitions get realized, and at such a young age, marriage can easily become a dead end for ambitious Indian girls. I also hope she has the chance to see some sights beyond Bangalore, and maybe one day to go abroad.

But I still have to marvel at her mother for trying so hard. If that perseverance has reached the daughter, she will go far.

Inspiration for the Journey

ॐ

After several weeks in my "new" Bangalore office, faces, if not names, became very familiar. Indian names are hard for Westerners because Indian names span the gamut of many languages, and often family surnames do not pass down to the children, particularly in South India. My seventh floor office, just on the end of the tarmac at Bangalore's city airport, housed some corporate functions, and some senior architects in our software group. There was a natural friendliness that developed between me and my new clients, driven by an interest in each others background, and the fact that we were all working for the same company, with common goals. It was an exciting time to be a part of the emerging Indian economy. In particular, I thoroughly enjoyed the melting pot of Bangalore, listening to many different languages, trying to figure out people's ancestral location based upon their last names, etc. I also enjoyed listening to different religious views, and slowly learning about the different Hindu deities represented in the cubicles around my office. And, we had free coffee and tea in the office in India, with a person to serve it. We certainly did not have that back in New York!

I had noticed the empty chair of one of my new colleagues, a software developer named Sateesh. He was always a welcoming, gentle helper for me in so many things. I remember him taking time shortly after my arrival to talk about different temple sites that I should visit nearby, and he was always willing to explain a religious practice in an even and balanced manner. Since we both were in the office early, and would catch up before the day got crazy, his absence became noticeable to me after several days, which melted into several weeks. When I asked about his whereabouts, people assumed he was on holiday, or as the Indians would say "he is out of station!" I still love those vestigial British phrases which the Indians use today.

Sateesh returned to the office after about a month. He had grown a beard, his hair was long and he was noticeably thinner. I was happy to see him, and catch up on his "vacation." I knew he was an avid hiker, and I figured he must have gone for a great trek somewhere, maybe up to the Himalayas.

Sateesh informed me that he was on vacation, but not trekking in the "leisure" sense. Instead, he was participating in an ecumenical brotherhood march in Kerala, to several well known Hindu temple destinations. The idea behind the brotherhood march was to gather together men of all religions, caste, background, economic means and livelihood in a show of solidarity for the sacredness of all people as brothers and sisters, just as they are. Walking and talking together, praying, eating together and helping the poor and struggling along the way was the method of breaking down barriers between people, and reducing the collaborative effort and material needs to only what was essential. This way, through the renunciation of the trappings of wealth, caste and even religious belief, God, Atman, Allah, and Buddha would all shine through for each individual. Each person helped his neighbor, whether it meant the infirm trying to get to the next temple location, or sharing a simple meal of rice and dal from a common plate. No alcohol, meat or tobacco was consumed by the pilgrims.

Sateesh told me that he tried to do this every year, and was joined by thousands from around India who made the same journey through Kerala at around the same time of the year. He encouraged me to join him if I could. He told me that this pilgrimage really helped him understand what it meant to be united as children of god. His face radiated a peacefulness that told me the pilgrimage achieved its goal.

On my way home I thought about how glad I was to see him. And how lucky I was to be in a place that employed people like Sateesh, who challenged my views of how the game of life should be played.

Forgiveness

ॐ

In an effort to try and give something to the people that had welcomed me so warmly to India, I began giving free guitar lessons to interested students, and some colleagues. One student in particular took to the guitar, having had some background in classical Hindustani instruments. He purchased a guitar willingly and practiced diligently. We were soon playing some western songs together and eventually got to the point of performing for a group of people after hours one day. He also taught me the Hindi words to a popular movie song that I play and sing to this day.

He was a very interesting guy, and we met only occasionally since he didn't live in the city. However, when we did meet, we could easily share stories, discuss philosophy and talk about life. He was a huge cricket fan, as are most Indians, and we would occasionally watch some games together on TV. I didn't care much for the game of cricket, simply due to a lack of understanding. My friend really tried to teach me the basics, which I soon grasped, although I never had the passion for the game that the locals do.

I recall one discussion in particular with Raju after watching some cricket. He relayed to me a personal story in which he felt convinced that a friend, indeed someone I knew, had betrayed him over a deeply personal matter. He was in a somber mood, and I knew that the pain was deep. I felt genuine concern for Raju, as our discussions were generally very fun and upbeat, and the mood had suddenly gone from lively to dark, and a bit sad.

Several days later we were having some tea together. As we often did, we slipped into a discussion about religion. He had a pretty deep understanding of Hinduism, and could easily compare and contrast world religions, including Islam, Buddhism and Christianity. He began to ask me my personal view of the "key" points of Christianity. He likely knew as much about the general precepts of Christian thought as I did, but we soon turned to the topic of forgiveness. I was talking about my own belief in Jesus as a merciful brother, more interested in the next positive steps we take, then in the wrong steps we have already taken. I told him about the Sacrament of Reconciliation in the Catholic Church, and how forgiveness for sins, absolution, actually provided me with a good deal of strength in my life. Christians believe that Jesus came to live among us and died for our sins, showing us the path to salvation by following his own simple path of loving one's neighbor. As I explained to Raju, forgiveness is the essential gift given to us by a loving God, enabling us to face another day with our eyes fixed forward, instead of on the list of past transgressions.

My friend thought about this for awhile, and in fact was silent for a few minutes. Suddenly, he began to get animated, began to smile and said "Yes, that is it! I haven't forgiven! This is what I need to do!"

I realized he was tying our previous discussion about the person who had betrayed him, and our current discussion on religion. And he was now talking about forgiving this person. It was as if a light went on for him. I was amazed to see a calm transform my friend, who seemed to have just found a path to move beyond his anger, which had really been getting the best of him. He was obviously focusing on ways to improve his own inner self, and rather then relying only on his own view, he was actually trying to draw from a religion not his own. It was equally incredible to me that someone experiencing this deep hurt would lay out his vulnerability, quite openly, and ask for help. Few of us have the humility of soul to seek out advice from a friend when it deals with a personal issue. We often see it as a sign of weakness to not have all the solutions in our own head. Somewhere, he had faith enough to talk about his problem, and hope that a solution might come forward.

It is this very openness to spiritual growth and discussion which Gandhi harnessed in his pursuit of Truth, and in mobilizing his followers. He said:

"I feel that India's mission is different from that of others. India is fitted for the religious supremacy of the world. There is no parallel in the world for the process of purification that this country has voluntarily undergone." Mahatma Gandhi – "Speeches and Writings of Mahatma Gandhi", 1933 Chennai.

I had just witnessed a modern day example of this spiritual growth, and still draw inspiration from that discussion.

A Taste of Paan

ॐ

I went out one day after work with a friend for dinner. He was about to leave our company to study some advanced computer concepts related to the medical profession at a foreign university. I wanted to take him out, knowing that I might not see him again for a long time. He was going far away, and was also leaving his mother behind. He had been a good friend, and as a Muslim, he was able to give me a perspective on Indian life that I enjoyed. He wasn't deeply religious however, and so we spoke less about spirituality per se, and more about the cultural happenings and the perceptions of different religious groups in India. For example, he told me that in India occasionally Muslims and Hindus would get under each other's skin. And sometimes worse. One could imagine that millions of people, in a hot place with high poverty and limited job opportunities can create an environment where tensions easily flare.

For example, he explained to me that Hindus would take great offence at the Muslim practice of butchering beef. While of course Muslims were under no religious prohibition against eating beef, the lack of sensitivity to the treatment of the cow could easily raise the ire of Hindus. Similarly, with Muslims congregating for prayer five times a day, in the quiet and simple setting of a mosque, some Hindus would seize this opportunity to practice their drums and brass bands outside the mosque at the "convenient" time. My friend could explain these situations to me with balance, facts and understanding, and his delivery was even on both sides of the story.

After our meal, he took me to his favorite "paan" stall on a nearby street. I had tried paan before. It is a sweet concoction of betel leaf with sweet pastes and spices wrapped all together in a chewable wad. I observed that Indians have a real sweet tooth, and after a spicy filling meal, a plug of paan would normally go well to aid digestion, and cleanse the palette as one strolled around the city. I would often see people spitting out bits and pieces of the paan as they worked it around in their mouths. This produced a less then attractive scene, as it was done openly, on the streets and usually straight ahead! But, that was the preferred method, and part of the culture. My friend wanted me to try his favorite place, and he asked me to wait to one side while he had his paan wallah (paan maker or deliverer) prepare a wad of the sweet mixture for me. I could hear a bit of back and forth going on, and some pointing at me, with the words "medium" spoken in English, but other than that, I couldn't make out the full discussion.

I soon had an extra large leafy paan in my mouth, and immediately began to enjoy the sweet nectar and satisfying chew of the experience. My friend looked on, clearly enjoying his own paan. In a minute or two, however, I began to experience a strange light- headed sensation. I backed off a bit, looking at my friend for an explanation, but I didn't spit out the paan since it was a special preparation for me. He began to smile, and almost laugh, as he told me that the paan I was chewing had tobacco in it… not much, just "medium." My head soon began to swim as I tried to work the tobacco laced "paan" to another side of my mouth.

Soon, I could feel some burning on the inside of my cheek, and found a place to spit out the wad. I had to sit down, and I needed water. I felt as if I had been hit by a truck.

I sat down on a stone fence near the paan stall with my head in my hands, trying to not fall down. My friend's little joke worked, and I guess he wanted to make sure that I wouldn't forget him! When I looked up, I saw 3 kids and some older men laughing and pointing at me from the paan stall. The man who made the pan was also now laughing fully, as was my friend.

I was waiting for the "candid camera" to come out. I'm sure I could have served as the poster boy for Gandhi's quote "Drugs and Drink are the two arms of the devil with which he strikes his helpless victims into stupefaction and intoxication." Young Indian, April 12, 1926. Most people do not take paan with tobacco; they simply enjoy the fresh leaf, some nuts and sweets. Unfortunately the night ended sooner for me then expected, as I hailed a rickshaw to go home to bed.

I guess the story of the foreigner who couldn't handle his paan has been told at that paan stall many times! I hope my legacy in India extended beyond that, but in retrospect, I'm glad to have served, albeit unwittingly, as a reason for laughter on the crowded street.

Making "paan" at a paan stall in Bangalore

Give me ten Rupees!

ॐ

Mysore is an attractive, airy city south of Bangalore. A commanding presence in the city is the ancestral palace of the King of Mysore, a magnificent, sprawling estate still well appointed and maintained as the most important tourist attraction in the city. In addition to the King's palace, there are several important summer homes which housed his attendants in the 18th and 19th centuries, as well as a large Catholic Cathedral (St. Philomena's), and some nice shady parks. Mysore is really a superb location in India, with a relatively cool climate, pleasant people and traces of British Raj era finery that conveys the opulence of the once phenomenally wealthy Princely states, some of which co-existed with the British Empire.

The palace itself is breathtaking. It has the largest crystal chandelier I have ever seen (even outdoing Versailles!). The last king of Mysore, who was basically unseated after India's partition in 1947, had a classical penchant for tiger hunts, cars, carriages and an amazing collection of record players and Victrolas. The King of Mysore was on relatively good terms with the British, who let his princely Kingdom march on more or less to its own devices. The King of Mysore was not stripped of royalty or forced out by the British, as long as he allowed Bangalore to serve as a garrison or cantonment area for the Empire. In addition, the King of Mysore was able to leverage his "friendship" with the Brits as a source of western goods with which to adorn his home. The black and white posed pictures of the King, shown hosting British and European dignitaries, always included scenes of opulent feasts, hunts, cars and his "privileged" children. In Bangalore, there is a summer palace still occupied by a descendant of the king. This "king," as he is still called, has devoted his time I'm told, to creating women's fashions, and collecting paintings of women, many of them nude, which are hung around the premises. The Bangalore palace grounds also serve as a forum for rock concerts and other large gatherings.

On a spiritual note, Mysore is also home to one of the seven "holy hills" of South India. Chamundi Hill is large, about 1000 meters tall, and is dedicated to one of the Indian goddesses, Chamundeshwari, who slew an evil demon in battle. It continues to be a very popular pilgrimage site, and there are several temples on the Hill itself, which can be reached by car, or on foot for the real devotee. In India, where God is viewed as being everywhere, but primarily inside you, many landforms, rivers and mountains like the Himalayas, or the Ganges, take on a holy meaning and significance. Visits to those areas bring blessings, and pujas, or blessing ceremonies by a Brahmin priest, are sought out to seek the God's favor. Chamundi Hill is such a place, and also offers a fabulous view of Mysore. From the top you can see the king's palace, the horse track, and feel the wonderful breeze that takes you out of the city swelter.

We decided to walk to the famous monolithic statute of Nandi. Nandi was the great bull of Lord Krishna who pulled his chariot during the epic battles described in Indian mythology. Nandi the bull is worshipped throughout India, and temples to Nandi generally contain a large granite carving of the bull, which is usually treated with oils and festooned with garlands. Food offerings, such as coconuts and bananas, are often offered to Nandi by both the casual worshippers and priests during the pujas.

Most Indian temple areas will have a makeshift marketplace outside where trinkets, handicrafts, food and other items are sold on blankets or in small kiosks. While one thinks back to Jesus' admonition of the money lenders and hawkers at the temple gates in Jerusalem, pilgrimage sites are considered areas of commerce in India. People travel long distances on bad roads to visit these holy sites. They have to eat, and the opportunity to make a little money or sell some items near a temple is not viewed as diminishing the sacred aura of the location. It is a good opportunity to find customers, who like to make a day of visiting a temple.

As a family of western travelers, we were quickly approached by some children who were a bit more industrious then the average street kids looking for a quick rupee. One young boy, confident and determined, approached us with the proposition that he could name the capitals of Europe, and would gladly do so in exchange for some rupees. I admired the perseverance of this boy, who had several others "in training" who would mimic his words, learn his delivery, and presumably one day ply their trade at other choice spots on Chamundi Hill. We accepted the deal and he began to rattle off Rome, Paris, Madrid, but he got a little stuck somewhere up in Scandinavia. To keep the sport going, I told him that he needed to get it right, and that we would come back after we had visited the temple.

Indian street kids in pursuit of a few rupees are not that easily thrown off! They have learned that you strike while the iron is hot, particularly when there are foreigners around, since foreigners, particularly Americans, represent about the only chance for a kid to make some easy money. We were thus pursued with increased determination, as the boys began to shout out "no sir, wait, Ahhsllloooo is Norway capital… Stockenhagen Is Sweden capital, I am right, I AM RIGHT! In the spirit of interacting with the kids, and knowing I would of course give them some money, I said "no, that is not correct. Stockholm is the capital of Sweden. You should now give me a rupee!"

To my amazement, this little boy reached into his pocket and actually handed me one rupee! While a rupee might only be around 2 cents, it nevertheless was money the boy had somehow earned, or found, or begged for. The little boy had a look of disappointment on his face, but seemed to believe that the game had to be played fairly, by the rules, and that somehow I was an authority figure and could request that he part with a rupee for failing to get the capitals all correct.

The gesture of this little boy, training others, so determined, and yet so willing to part with his money was touching indeed. We rehearsed the capitals again, and I made sure that the little band of capital experts had it straight. When they did, they earned their money, and confidently set off for the next group of western tourists.

Had I not stayed for two years in India, my tolerance for such episodes would have been much less. I hope that these kids are given the opportunity one day to see the world beyond Chamundi Hill, and maybe travel to the capitals that they had learned by heart. Most of all, I continue to marvel at their perseverance and determination. Imagine the students they would be if given the chance!

Mysore Palace

Darjeeling Tea farms

ॐ

In our fast paced world of equally fast food, drive through oil changes, and Starbucks, we don't often think about the source of our food. We know it is grown (or chemically combined!) somewhere, and that people or machines package it and send it to our stores. We mostly know the branding and marketing of the food and its packaging. We could likely pick our favorite brand off the shelf simply based on the "look and feel" of the label. For Americans, a box of Cheerios, or a jar of Hellmans' mayonnaise, or Green Giant canned vegetables is an easy example. Even if you couldn't make out the words on the label, you could likely pick it out from the other items on the shelves. Yes, marketing does work!

Did you ever stop to think about those people in distant lands who really grow the food, and cultivate the land, and ultimately harvest the item, particularly the fruits and vegetables? Where are they, and what is their life like? What do they look like, and do I see a connection between them and me? Do I appreciate their labor as I consume the food they have harvested? What kinds of choices do they have in their lives? Do they even get to consume the food that they grow? What are their wages, how do they live, and do they ever get time off? Do I ever think about "fairness" in all of this? Is there anything I can do about it? Big questions that could take volumes to explore.

I had the most remarkable experience in Darjeeling visiting the tea farms which line the hills and valleys of this North Indian city, in the foothills of the Himalayas. Darjeeling straddles the border of Nepal, Sikkim (now India, but if you ask the Chinese, it is China!) and Bhutan. The city and distant mountains are so incredibly beautiful, so breathtaking, that you could easily miss the tea farms all around. Most of us have heard about "Darjeeling tea," but I had never even thought about a tea farm. When seen in April or May, during the moist season of the northern monsoon, the hills are lined with endless deep green jewels, which are really tea bushes with smallish bright green leaves that clump together in short shrubs, maybe 3-4 feet across. From a distance, they really do look like emeralds against the mountainsides, neatly laid out. And around Darjeeling, the tea plantations are huge, go on for acres, and seem to provide work for many, mostly women, during the harvest season.

If you are lucky and visit the tea farms during this time of year, you will see hundreds, maybe thousands of women, in either traditional saris with a smock over them, or, in some cases, Tibetan garb, long colorful skirts and hats. Everyone has a large basket on their back, and although I have not picked tea leaves, the process seems slow going, and time consuming. The idea is that you have to find the leaves when they are just right.....and certain bushes might have a varying palette of colors which require some hunting around to get to the choicest tea leaves.

Looking at a mountainside at harvest time, all these women are interspersed across the hills, bent over, and picking tea leaves. From a short distance, their random presence on different parts of the mountain breaks up the otherwise uniform rows of tea bushes. When their basket is full, or when there is a break, they come into the processing plant in a long line walking slowly, or by truck load, where they sit in the back of a pickup truck with their precious cargo. One thing I find remarkable about most cultivation in India is how quiet things are. No machine is used to pick the tea off the bushes. The women appear to be at the top of the world, with hawks flying around, often in oppressive heat, with the sacred Himalaya Mountains in the distance. I suppose it would be a good place to pray quietly as you worked, if you could clear your mind from your work.

When the women come in from the fields, they are largely silent. You don't hear them joking around, like men might at a construction site. I don't recall hearing them talk much at all as they emptied their baskets into the large holding containers just outside the processing facility. They looked tired, serious. Out picking tea, they probably have a lot of time to think about their families in the fields, what they would need to cook for dinner, or about getting some rest. What about a sick child, or the fact that they might have been in pain from the back breaking work they were doing? They probably have very little time to think about themselves. They didn't look angry, but they did look tired.

Some took a second to notice the faces of the foreigners in their midst as they walked in to deposit their basket of tea leaves. It always amazed me how simply the presence of some foreigners would bring smiles to the faces of Indian laborers and villagers. I'm quite sure it had much to do with the strangeness of our clothing, the difference in skin or hair color, and maybe the fact that we all had cameras and were snapping pictures and wearing funny hats. Maybe that was a short enough diversion for them. I was happy to see some of them smile. But something deep down told me that while their smiles came easily, and were sincere, "smiling" and "feeling good" was not the primary purpose or goal in their lives.

Inside the factory, some more women, and now some men, were engaged in sifting, drying, and inspecting the tea leaves. Others were building wooden boxes, by hand, to ship the tea, and painting stencils on the boxes to show the type of tea and quality of the tea. Some machines assisted in these tasks. Certain precious leaves, called "silver tips," were segregated and handled with great care as they were supposed to be the cream of the crop. We had a short tour in which we watched the various stages of the drying and packaging process. Again, this was not a particularly jovial factory environment. The work was largely done in quiet.

As I spent more time in India, I learned that this was not a sign of discontent, or sadness. As Americans, we always seem to connect silence with some problem......"You're so quiet, what's wrong?" I learned over time that the people of Darjeeling were made up of diverse mountain populations. Nepalese, Tibetans, Sikkimese mixed in with local Bengali's. In my travels, I have learned that mountain people, in general, tend to be more quiet then coastal people. I would like to think that part of the reason here is the breathtaking view of the Himalaya Mountains, which would easily put people at a loss for words. But again, I knew that most of the women were tired. Their duty and goals were different. They were not seeking thrills in their lives, or diversion from everyday activities.

Being an Indian woman from a village, working in the fields, then having to cook and clean, care for parents and in-laws as well as husbands and children, is among the hardest jobs in the world. These faces told a story of duty, of dignity and of purpose. I was so glad that the person making sample cups of tea for the visiting tourists was a man. The women were working hard enough already. When I have a cup of tea these days, I think of this connection to the women of the Darjeeling tea farms.

I bought about a pound of the Darjeeling tea straight from the farm, likely hand picked by the faces that I saw on that day. The tea is now pretty dried out, but I still sprinkle a few leaves in my tea about once a week from that farm. I wish I could confront the work God needs me to do with the same serenity, and dignity as those women of Darjeeling.

Workers bring in tea leaves from the tea plantations of
Darjeeling

An Indian Wedding

ॐ

Not long after I arrived in Bangalore, I found a beautifully decorated envelope on my chair at work one day. Inside was a wedding invitation, elegantly written in English and Tamil, requesting my "presence" at the wedding of a co-worker, a young woman who had been exceedingly helpful to me in getting things organized during my first few hectic weeks. The invitation had a picture of Lord Ganesh, the remover of obstacles, and some ornate lanyard-type decoration holding the multicolored pages together. I did not realize that most wedding invitations were hand carried into work and placed on desks, rather than sent via regular mail. There were many invitations on the desks in the office, reflecting the wonderful Indian view that celebrations are open for all.

I immediately walked over to my co-worker to congratulate her, and to tell her that I would be honored to attend. I was really very excited, since this wedding would be my first deep immersion into a religious/cultural event in India. She was equally excited, and told me that her family would love to have me there. I would have to be in Chennai, previously called Madras, for two days. The celebration dinner was scheduled during the evening, and the wedding puja (blessing service) was scheduled for early the next day. Why two days? Because the astrologer who had been consulted had selected the day after the party, at the exact time of 7:30am, as the auspicious time for the nuptials. The auspicious time was based upon the astrologer's reading of the planetary movements at the time of the birth of the bride and groom. Such consultations are common for Hindus, both in and outside of India. It only then hit me that Chennai was 300 miles away! I decided to go by train to Chennai from Bangalore, which would provide me with a glimpse of the main transportation system across state borders in India. Indian Railways is still a great source of pride for India. It is also the largest single employer in the country.

I booked a ticket in an air conditioned car, which left at 6am for the 6 hour trip. The train was more or less an express, stopping at only five locations inside Tamil Nadu, the state in which Chennai is located. On the outside of the train car was a neat check-in sheet, with my name and assigned seat number listed in alphabetical order. A very well spoken gentleman's voice welcomed us all in English over the loudspeaker to the Shatabji Line, direct from Bangalore to Chennai. Soon after, a well groomed conductor in smart, military style uniform came by to collect our tickets and ensure things were in order.

To my great surprise and delight, coffee and breakfast were served on the train. The coffee in India always tasted great to me, perhaps because it was locally grown, and prepared sweet and creamy. Breakfast was a warm masala dosa (a light, fresh cooked thin bread crepe stuffed with seasoned potato and onions), some toast and jam, and some juice. As day broke, and we started to get into rural areas, and I again marveled at how hard Indians worked their fields and the land. The dirt roads and small dwellings, the children running around playing in little streams, the dogs and the livestock from my window view were my traveling companions. I received many stares whenever I stuck my head out the window at the local stops.

After getting off the train, I needed to get to the pre-booked hotel which the bride had arranged for visiting guests. I was happy that it had an air conditioning window unit, as Chennai is notoriously hot, humid and can be quite buggy. I arrived hoping for an in-room ironing board as my "wedding" clothes had been crushed hastily inside my luggage. As none was to be found, I had to wear a light sweater over a very wrinkled shirt, which alone caused me to lose about 3 pounds during the sweltering evening. The evening weather was true Chennai, very hot and very humid! I was finally able to communicate the location of the reception hall to a non- English, non- Hindi speaking rickshaw driver, and I luckily arrived in time for greeting the bride and groom, their families, and other guests before dinner started.

I will never forget how exotic, at least for me, this event was on that evening on the outskirts of Chennai. The wedding hall was full of lights, with a huge floral sign welcoming guests to the wedding of Chitra and Dinesh. Some classical Tamilian music was being played live by musicians sitting on a carpet on the floor, including the captivating drone of the sitar and its pulsating tabla (drum) accompaniment. There was also a clarinet–like woodwind instrument (probably the same instrument used by the snake charmers) being played expertly, and I couldn't help but hang around the musicians as others chatted away mostly in Tamil. Indeed, I was not only the only foreigner at the wedding, but for some of the older relatives, maybe one of the few they had seen. The kids in particular took a great interest in me, with many coy little ones hiding behind chairs and tables, only to catch a look at the strange man in the sweater, and then hide again. Luckily, I could talk to the children who were generally going to English medium schools.

I was anticipating, in fact, the sort of crazy Indian wedding scene reminiscent of the popular movie "Monsoon Wedding," with lots of people dancing, arms up in the air, heavy thumping to the beat of bollywood music, and lots of liquid refreshment to keep the party going. I was exhausted, thirsty, and was hoping for at least a cold beer. As I began to survey the scene it occurred to me that most people were sitting around, talking, having some snacks, and relaxing. Pictures were being taken of the wedding party, and certainly the people in attendance were kind enough and friendly.

But there was no beer or wine to be found. It was then that I spied a co-worker who had made the trip from Bangalore, and she began to explain that south Indian weddings are not the crazy, dancing, drinking, heavy music events found in the North in Punjab and Dehli. Rather, the Tamil Brahmins (highest caste Hindus) are generally considered the guardians of Hindu culture, and purity. These were vegetarian, no- alcohol or tobacco affairs, where the emphasis was on tradition and culture and spirituality. Indeed, the explanation came with almost a certain disdain for the "wild" north Indian ways. I began to conjure up the analogy of a wedding in a bible belt dry county in the South part of the U.S., versus a big Irish shindig in New York or Boston.

We had a very tasty traditional vegetarian "thali," with people sitting in rows together, using a large clean green banana leaf as a plate. Attendants served various rice and vegetarian dishes, followed by sweets and "paan" (nuts and sweet pastes wrapped in betel leaf). After dinner, I went back to the larger reception hall. Some dance music was starting to come over the load speakers, largely Hindi movie tunes, and more surprises were in store for me! Several of the children got up, including one young boy who was particularly bold, and they began to dance choreographed routines from some clearly famous films. I think I was the only one who didn't know the words or moves.

One young boy had on his dark glasses, was whipping his hair back, and posing with a cool, far away look that really made me laugh. Next, several men got up, all dancing together and having a great time. I looked around at the collection of very pretty women still seated, talking amongst themselves, and realized that they had no intention of dancing. This was something the men did! I learned that it is not particularly dignified for women in sari's to dance, let alone with men, and for the rest of my two years in India I marveled at this culture in which the men dance together. I was soon asked to join (my foot tapping and general feel for the beat clearly gave me away!), and I tried, hard as it was, to move comfortably around the dance floor in my sweater, dripping wet, and surrounded by other men, all of whom were smiling and pushing me on.

I went back to the hotel, exhausted from the long day, was attacked by mosquitos all night long, and could not wait for part two of the Indian wedding – the puja service itself!

Luckily, the astrologers picked 7:30 am for the beginning of the puja service, so I could get out of bed early, shower and count up my mosquito bites. At the service itself there were many recitations from ancient Sanskrit verses, lots of symbols, decorations, and real beauty to behold. I approached a sage looking older gentleman, and enquired as to what was going on at a particular part of the service, and he said he really didn't know. Not many of the people could follow the dialog, but some said that in general, the bonds of matrimony were being established, and the blessings were being implored for prosperity, health, and children. The couple was tied together by a string, as a sign of their bond, which would become a gold necklace for the bride after several weeks or months.

I noticed, in stark contrast to Western Christian weddings, that there was no "kiss the bride," no open display of affection, and not much by way of smiling going on in general by bride and groom. Hindu brides traditionally don't smile, as historically they are cut away from their parents at the time of the marriage, and generally go off to their husband's households. This couple was a bit more progressive, and they would be moving back to Bangalore… without parents.

In reflecting on the arranged marriage, the sense of duty that goes with marriage and the centuries old traditions in Indian weddings where love does not enter into the selection, it occurred to me that perhaps the Hindus had some real insight into what makes a marriage last. Most Indian couples learn to love each other because they work together for their common good, provide for their children, and seek to carry out their dharma, their duty, as husband and as wife. Our western notions of "love at first sight" and Hollywood romance, which are centered on self-fulfillment, and the idea that one needs to be "swept off their feet," do not play a part in sustaining the relationship generally in Hindu marriages. The divorce rate is very low in Hindu circles, and based on what I saw, these couples are as content as any others. One other bond that likely keeps the marriage in place is the extensive support (which westerners could find stifling) of the extended family, and its role in reinforcing the obligations and responsibilities of the couple to parents, in-laws, and other relatives.

I learned so much at this wedding in Chennai. Both bride and groom are happy, hard working, and have just had their first child. They did not need lots of fanfare and lavish parties to celebrate their union. No one needed to parade around in a spectacle, and no one recounted drunken stories of the reception. They know their duty to each other and their families. They have received their blessings from well wishers and the Brahmin priest officiating. They now go off to live their lives, and work hard to fulfill their responsibility to each other. The couple wants to do what is right, according to their tradition. I'm quite sure they will spend many years together.

Do not commit nuisance!!

ॐ

We expect to be surprised when traveling abroad by incredible architecture, odd vehicles, different clothing styles and often, food. Yet at time the most disarming encounters are those personal habits of a people, or culture, which challenge our own deeply engrained views of right and wrong, clean or dirty, fun or annoying. India is full of such contrasts, and most Americans tend to marvel initially at the presence of cows or even temple elephants walking leisurely around crowded city streets. We want to say "Wow, do you see that cow over there? "Indians would find nothing interesting in this at all, since, of course, cows do roam freely on the streets in India.

I recall early in my assignment to Bangalore seeing a lovely yellow sign on a stone wall which enclosed a school in one of the older sections of town. It was a market area, and the sign was a cement placard in which the following words were neatly inscribed - "Committing Nuisance here is Prohibited." I was intrigued by the sign, not simply because I wasn't sure what it meant, but because the same words were also inscribed in Kannada, whose lovely circle-like letters ensured that I would never learn the local language, and Urdu, whose Arabic script told me that I was in an area with a sizeable Muslim culture. Had Hindi been on the sign, it would have been a perfect linguistic representation of the language situation in Bangalore.

Indian languages, with their exotic scripts, flourishing and intertwining like wildflowers in a field, fascinate me. In Bangalore, four languages could be heard to a varying extent. The most common language is English, the legacy of the British Empire in India, and likely the most important legacy for the Indian economy. Next is Kannada, an ancient and classical language of the Karnataka state in south India, whose speakers still number tens of millions, but whose language, as a source of local pride and literature, is somewhat under threat by English. Next, you might find Urdu, that linguistic hybrid of Hindi and Persian (Farsi) that is spoken largely in Muslim circles in India and Pakistan, and which employs the Arabic script. Finally, there is Hindi, which is technically the national language of India. The use of Hindi in India was an attempt to unify the country after Independence with a native Indian language, instead of English, which was seen as the language of the occupying British. Hindi is used in government and spoken throughout the north of the country, but of limited penetration in day to day conversation in the south of India. In fact, in the state of Tamil Nadu, little Hindi is employed in day to day conversation, and most locals will not use the language unless absolutely necessary.

It did not take me long to understand what the sign was driving at!! Indian cities lack basic access to public restrooms and toilets for most of the population not working in an area with plumbing. Without going too deeply here, most people living in villages and rural areas need not worry particularly about access to a clean lavatory, as forests, parks and fields generally provide adequate shelter to modestly answer nature's call. In India, the situation is a bit more exasperating for women, as modesty in the culture requires women generally to be completely hidden during their private time.

However, in Indian cities, to which substantial millions of rural workers have flocked over the last hundred years, the absence of both public facilities and trees has created a bit of a problem. Most workers and laborers literally have nowhere to "go" when the need arises. Most people employed on the streets as sweepers, hawkers, and rickshaw drivers are not office workers, and like many other laborers, they do not have a "home base" for relieving themselves. Private residences and commercial establishments are often delineated by cement walls or other fencing in India, both to protect and to ensure that "rights of admission" are reserved; so many main streets are lined with walls that can stretch for blocks and blocks. In fact Bangalore, in its city center and cantonment area, has more fencing and walls guarding compounds then many other cities in India because the British tended to wall off their canteens, army garrisons, parade grounds and parks. As one can imagine, a busy worker on a street is left with very few options when nature calls in between deliveries, or while waiting forever for a bus.

Most municipalities in the West have regulations against public urination. One will not find a person relieving themselves on Fifth Avenue or the Champs Elysee without the assistance of the local police. In many cities in India, however, you will see men urinating on an outdoor wall or fence, next to a busy sidewalk or near a "flyover" (bridge) in relatively full and open glory. Little effort is made to hide oneself while in the act, and indeed, several men can often be seen relieving themselves while in casual conversation, without the least bit of attention being paid to the passersby a yard or two away. Thankfully, most such offenders do offer the courtesy of turning their backs toward the passing public. Similarly, the rest of the populace moves on briskly, without notice or apparent concern, presumably with an understanding that those caught in the act have few options.

Some women might even hide a bit of envy, since the men don't have to hold it forever, or journey a mile away to one of the few public women's toilets.

Westerners are pretty shocked to see this display on first arrival. I have heard people say "why don't they find somewhere else to go to the bathroom," or "That is really gross" and "what kind of place doesn't have a restroom for people to use?" We forget that most Westerners do have the luxury of a relatively clean bathroom when away from home, as every restaurant and most stores provide a facility for their customers as a courtesy. Over time, my own senses were dulled to the men openly "committing nuisance" on public streets. If you are there long enough, as I was, you begin to not only understand the problem itself, but you might find yourself employing the remedy as well!

One day, however, I was struck by the comic irony of a particular sight. I was passing a government air force residence in the middle of town, one of many subsidized residential colonies for armed forces workers and officers. On the wall was a standard "anti-nuisance" sign. To be completely accurate, I should point out that occasionally the word "no urination" is required to be used, as it is now a good 60 years since the British occupied India, and fewer ordinary people understand the euphemism of "committing nuisance" any more. Within 3 yards of the sign itself, which repeated every 30 feet or so, an air force guard was marking his territory, so to speak, on the very wall prohibiting the commission of such "nuisance!" I'm sure he had to go, didn't get a break for several hours, and had little choice in the matter.

I don't have a solution to the anti-nuisance conundrum in India. While it is certainly disarming at first to see people on crowded streets relieving themselves, the necessity for such activity is understandable. Gandhi himself railed against unsanitary conditions, on the basis of its ability to spread disease. He always required his ashram dwellers to keep an organized latrine, away from the living area, and fastidious personal cleanliness to promote hygiene.

In Gandhi's view, outer cleanliness reflected inner holiness.

I'm not sure how India will deal with this issue over time. It may remain one of those aspects of Indian city life that continues to challenge the western traveler. The fact is that there is not a lot of extra money in the Indian budgets to fund public toilets. And historically and culturally, building toilets in a city has never been a priority. I was glad, however, that I remained in India long enough to come to an understanding of the problem, to erase my initial conclusions and prejudices, and to gain some insight into some of the basic challenges that India, and half of the world for that matter, confront in day to day living.

The Dance Village and Rock Pub

ॐ

On a hot July day we traveled with some friends about 20 kilometers outside of Bangalore to a "dance village," where students from around India are trained in various forms of Indian classical dancing. The place was hard to find and required the navigation of several long dirt roads and thousands of potholes - those classic Indian road potholes which will never get fixed and simply become obstacles that you maneuver around. The kids loved the impromptu bouncing carnival ride in the backseat as we drove over the holes and bumps.

The dance village, called Nrityagram, is actually a series of clay huts and performance venues, situated in a beautiful garden setting where wild flowers and vegetables are grown, largely for the consumption of the people studying there. The deceiving entrance sign is an impressive arch, which then leads to an understated, stark and almost religious atmosphere that is earthy and more functional then decorative. We entered the shady grounds, and I was immediately taken by the stillness of the place, which is ordinarily a good sign in India, except when you are expecting to see a dance show starting in 30 minutes! As it turned out, there was a miscommunication, and while the dancers ordinarily practice at the time of day indicated, they were traveling and performing shows outside of India on that day. When I asked the young woman where the dancers were, she showed me a schedule hanging on a board outside the main ticket office door. The schedule, to my great surprise, indicated that they were in the United States, in fact, not far from my home state of Connecticut. This got a good bit of laughter from our visiting friends from Connecticut, who were a little concerned that their three boys would find anything remotely interesting in watching an Indian cultural dance. At least there were some things to climb on for them.

I subsequently went back to Nrityagram, at a time when at least a few of the dancers were practicing. I was really amazed at the incredible dedication taken by these female students to study these ancient forms of dance. I was in luck that particular day, as the students were practicing a form of dance from Orissa, one of the states on the Eastern coast of India just south of Calcutta. The Orissi dance features a fair amount of "rhythmic "stomping on a wooden floor. The dancers are made up with heavy black eye liner, which highlights their sideways look as they position their hands in various graceful poses, moving their head horizontally… or so it appears!

In fact, the hand poses alone are many, are exact, and require significant concentration and practice in and of themselves. In the practice room, a woman beating out a rhythm on a wooden block was joined by another teacher carefully scrutinizing every move being made by the students. I think I saw a particular hand gesture repeated at least 20 times during a 15 minute glimpse of the practice session. Never had I seen such concentration on a student's face, as the dancer, I would say around 20 years old, strained to precisely copy the gentle hand waving motion that the teacher was imparting.

This was not a simple hobby. These girls had left their homes to train with some of the best classical dance teachers in India, lived in relatively austere conditions, and practiced their craft with the conviction of religious practice. In fact, the Orissi dance forms largely derive from the dancing of the temple girls a thousand years ago. Apparently there came a time when this was frowned upon, with boys substituting as dancers in the temple areas. It seems that a resurgence of this dance form has taken place in the last 60 years or so. Unfortunately, again I had missed the chance to see the full dance performance. But this glimpse has sparked an interest which I hope to have many years to explore, especially since the Orissi dancers make stops near my home in the US.

Just as Indians place great stock in their "holy men", saddhus and gurus, there is also a great reverence for the classical traditions, whether dance, singing or instrumental interpretation. Indeed, luckily for me, musical connections were easy to make. Bangalore is a place where modern western musical traditions, including rock music and jazz, truly thrive. As a guitarist and vocalist, I had several occasions during my stay in India to join with Indian's on stage performing live music. It was really fun for me to contribute a little bit to the wonderful exploration of culture that Indians cherish.

One day I was on business in Mumbai, and my cellphone rang as I was about to leave for the airport to return to Bangalore. It was a call from a local pub, called "The Legends of Rock" in Bangalore. They had a band cancel that evening, and based on a prior visit, where I played a few songs during the main performer's break, the owner of the club had called me and asked if I would fill in. I had no guitar, no amps or sound system, no music... - and was hundreds of miles away! I told him "sure"......... and begin to write out a short set list on the plane from the songs I had in my head based on 35 years of guitar playing and singing.

When I arrived 5 minutes before my set was to begin, I was shocked. There were posters, with ME on the wall, and hand out postcards which read "A New Yorker in Bangalore… Bob Carlsen." There was a good sized crowd in the audience for a small place in the middle of the week. I played the best of Simon and Garfunkel, James Taylor, Beatles, and other well known sing along songs. The crowd was mixed with younger IT professionals and a handful of people in their mid 50's. I could hear them singing along to Dire Straits and Rolling Stones. I decided to launch into a Hindi song to close the set out, called "Roobaru," made popular by the Hindi movie "Rang de Basanti." I needed a friend to hold the words, which I never succeeded in memorizing. But no one could tell the difference since the entire place knew the words, sung them loudly and made up for my many Hindi shortcomings.

This was a magical evening for me. The cultural landscape of India goes on for millions of miles, from classical dance to bollywood, to modern western songs, to Hindustani classical violin. Whether at the dance village, or the Legends of Rock, music and the arts bring people together to communicate in ways that form strong bonds of brotherhood and deep personal connections. I was offered a regular job at the Legends, but knew that I could not keep a steady commitment there with work and travel.

I was amazed to hear almost every word of American Pie being sung back at me in that crowded pub. I left knowing that a little bit of effort, an open mind, and the welcoming spirit of India create far more connections then separations in this amazingly diverse land.

Some Reflections on
Hinduism and Gandhi

ॐ

Hinduism is an extremely intricate religion, or more precisely, "way of life," which scholars believe has evolved over almost 3000 years through the clashing of several different cultures in India. I say "way of life," instead of religion because Hinduism does not fit easily into our western view of religious practice. In the US, we tend to view religious practice as a series of community based events, like Church on Sunday at a set time, receiving communion in a group, or attending a funeral as community. A central tenant of religions like Christianity, Judaism and Islam is the focus on a "community of believers." In these faiths, communal proclamation of the Word, and common prayer, strengthen the faith of those in the group, and give support and inspiration to spiritually weaker members.

Conversely, Hindu belief seeks to unite the individual with God (Atman), through individual practices of holiness, renunciation and meditation. While there are some common "practices" or approaches, like vegetarianism, or cow worship, which are basic elements of the Hindu belief system, the central goal of Hinduism is to find God inside yourself. Most Hindus would agree that this sacred path is really your own private journey, and is not dependent on a community of believers. Of course, sages, gurus and priests provide the necessary interpretations and ritual settings to keep one on the "inner path;" but ultimately, the believer chooses the path, set of practices and worship times which are best suited to finding the Divine inside oneself.

Hinduism does not trace its origin to a single point of revelation, or a flash in time when God made himself known as the true God. In contrast, Christians, Jews and Muslims believe that God called Abraham, at a fixed point in time, to found a great nation of followers. Like most spiritual paths, Hinduism seeks to answer the "eternal question," namely, what is the link between the individual soul and the ultimate, or Absolute, the Divine? Most Western religions and traditions approach this question with hands raised heavenward, and eyes turned upward to find the source of this revelation from "above." Hinduism, like Buddhism, turns its focus "inward" to find God. Enlightenment is the goal of Hinduism, and many practices, like yoga, meditation, fasting and prayer make up the process to find the "inner light," the Divine that is "inside" all of us. The earliest Hindu religious texts, the Vedas, describe the divine journey of man as follows:

"Find the eternal object of your quest within your soul; Enough have you wandered during the long period of your quest! At last when you turn your gaze inward, suddenly you realize that the bright light of faith and lasting truth was shining around you..... your searching mind at last finds the object of the search within your own heart and your inner vision is illuminated by this new realization" (from Yajur Veda 32. 11, as translated in "Saddhus," by Dolf Hartsuiker).

It is this inward focus which gives much of India its reflective or meditative character. We speak of India as a "spiritual place," because one easily finds this characteristic of searching for the internal balance in people. In India, despite the large number of temples everywhere, most of the spiritual activity is going on "inside" the individual (at least in the more rigorous practice of Hinduism), instead of in community as common in the West. That said, as in any religion, external practices cannot fully reveal the disposition of the heart. During my time in Bangalore, I knew many co-workers who would go to a temple, make an offering, visit the holy Ganges, or have a "puja" ceremony to try and get a favorable disposition of God towards a given aim or goal. For example, many, many students and their parents would increase their temple visits and offerings during exam times to try and cover the bases. In addition, there is also in practice a large intersection between Hinduism and astrology. Some people see this as a co-mingling of religion and superstition. However, meditation, prayer, fasting and yoga are not easily susceptible to flashy or hypocritical display, and in general, their proponents are people who are trying to lead holy lives.

Many have described Hinduism as "polytheistic," a religion which venerates thousands of gods, represented by statues, paintings and devotions. But in fact, for the Hindu, there is really only one Divine presence, "Atman", which manifests itself in many forms (deities) at the service of worshippers to deal with life's needs and requirements. In order to begin the inner journey to find God inside oneself, Hindu's believe that one largely needs to renounce the outer world, the material world. This is not unlike the mystical aspects of Judaism or Christianity, which also put great emphasis on quiet time and prayer, but in Hinduism, renunciation can become quite a bit more extreme. To this day it is not uncommon for Saddhus, or holy men, to wander naked, completely dependent on God to provide for their needs while they walk their inner journey.

Hindus also believe that God exists in all things, and especially in nature. The original spiritual writings of Hinduism, the Vedas, actually derive from the observations of the early sages, or "rishis" who sought a "cosmic" understanding of the world and its order.

Thus, in the normal progression of spiritual life for ancient Hindus, a man would leave his family and worldly concerns in his old age, and take to the jungle, to meditate on God. For devout Hindus, the ultimate bliss is found in cutting through earthly concerns, cares and influences, to find that source of life which is present inside all living beings. Passionless action according to duty, not concern on the ultimate success or failure of the act, is most important.

Renunciation and detachment are approached very practically in Hinduism, and great emphasis is placed on self control, and a lack of concern for those many events and circumstances which occur "outside," and over which most of us have no control. For some, self control – which assists in the ability to keep oneself focused on the inner light, is practiced through the renunciation of tobacco, alcohol, and even sexual activity. Gandhi's own thoughts on self control are revealing:

"The path of self-purification is hard and steep. To attain to perfect purity one has to become absolutely passion-free in thought, speech and action. To rise above the opposing currents of love and hatred, attachment and repulsion." (Gandhi – The Story of My Experiments with Truth.) "Nothing but ruin stares a nation in the face that is a prey to the drink habit. History records that empires have been destroyed through that habit. … Sex urge is a fine and noble thing. There is nothing to be ashamed of in it. But it is meant only for the act of creation. Any other use of it is a sin against God and humanity." Gandhi, the Harijan, 28, March 1936.

Gandhi himself, after some years of marriage and children, took the ultimate vow of "brahmacharya," complete abstinence from sexual relations, while still in his prime. While there had always been a path among Hindu sages to take this vow as the straight road to "self realization" through control, an incident in Gandhi's early years certainly planted the seed in this direction. He recounted in his autobiography that he was married at the very young age of 13, and he was quite taken by lustful desires with his equally young wife Kasturbai. Some years later, his father was on his deathbed. Gandhi had been attending to him in the family house, but asked an attendant to stay with his father while he went upstairs to spend some intimate time with his wife. Upon his return, his father had expired. Gandhi's grief was real and lasted the rest of his life. For Gandhi, this episode likely grew into his vow of total sexual abstinence later in life.

For Hindus, self control clears the path to train the mind on God. Again, in Gandhi's words, "All sins are committed in secrecy. The moment we realize that God witnesses even our thoughts we shall be free." The Harijan, 17, Jan. 1939. He goes on to say "control over thought is a long and painful and laborious process. But I am convinced that no time, no labor and no pain is too much for the glorious result to be reached. The purity of thought is possible only with a faith in God bordering on definite experience." Gandhi, Young Indian, 25 Aug. 1927.

Prayer and truth were the pillars of Gandhi's ideals. He spent hours in prayer each day, and one day a week in complete silence to focus his thoughts, quiet his mind and rid himself of distractions. Gandhi also studied a great deal about other religions, including Christianity. He was fascinated and drawn towards the Sermon on the Mount, and in fact seriously thought about becoming a Christian. Yet, he felt that he was most comfortable as a Hindu, and could carry out his life's works best by following the Gita, by fasting, by gaining control over his desires, and thus seeing the Truth clearly. Gandhi wrote, "What did Buddha do, and Christ do, and also Mohammed? Theirs were lives of self sacrifice and renunciation. Buddha renounced every worldly happiness because he wanted to share with the whole world his happiness, which was to be had by man who sacrificed and suffered in search for Truth." Young India 8 Dec. 1927.

And to what "Truth" did Gandhi commit himself? He sought the return of India to its ancient principles, simplicity, and self rule. His guiding principle in leading the non-violent struggle to rid India of 300 years of British rule was consistently based in a great faith that the British would come to see, by themselves, that they were wrong to control India. Gandhi believed that the British would not need to be defeated, or urged to leave by force; Rather, Gandhi felt that the British would leave voluntarily because their wrongdoing, when shown to them in the full light of Truth, would be condemnation enough.

However, after 300 years of British authority and ideas in India, many Indians had fully adopted western ways, and indeed, believed that the western ways, and even the English language, were the best. If India was weak, and its people were poor, it must be because they did not have the education of the West, the technology of the West, and so imitation of the West suited many in India. This is the environment in which Gandhi found himself.

Swami Vivekananda was another visionary Hindu who was a part of the renaissance of Hindu awakening in the later part of the 19th Century. He traveled widely, lectured in the United States, and is viewed as one of the pre-eminent spiritual leaders of Modern India. Like Gandhi, Vivekananda sought to galvanize India through recognition of self worth, and self determination. His commentary on the British makes the point:

"On one side, new India is saying, "If we only adopt western ideas, western language, western food, western dress, and western manners, we shall be strong and powerful as the western nations; on the other, old India is saying "Fools! By imitation others ideas never become one's own; nothing, unless earned, is your own. Does the ass in the lion's skin become the lion? On one side, new India is saying, "What the western nations do is surely good, otherwise how did they become so great?" On the other side, old India is saying, "the flash of lightening is intensely bright, but only for a moment; look out boys, it is dazzling your eyes. Beware! "Vivekananda follows up with "Social life in the West is like a peal of laughter; but underneath, it is a wail. It ends in a sob. The fun and frivolity are all on the surface: really it is full of tragic intensity. Now here (in India), it is sad and gloomy on the outside, but underneath are carelessness and merriment." See Vivekanda, His Call to the Nation, pgs. 261-62..

With a population in India that is about 83 percent Hindu, and an ancient belief that the Indian subcontinent was intended to be a Hindu cradle, there is no question that Hinduism can reach its long arm into politics. Several political parties represent Hindu beliefs, and the return to a Hindu India alone. These views can find their way into the workplace and into many other aspects of public life. No one is ashamed at the display of religion in India, and when it becomes a source of conflict, particularly with Muslims or occasionally Christians, there are ample voices in today's India to offer a calming return to brotherhood. And there are certainly enough statues of Mahatma (Great Soul) Gandhi to keep a watchful eye on people, challenging them with Truth.

Like all religions, if everyone practiced them in both spirit and deed, our world would be in more perfect balance, we would care more for each other then for things, and no doubt we would be more at peace. We would also likely have less, share more, shun meaningless technologies and gadgets, and perhaps work fewer hours.

India is caught in this pendulum today, with voices of the new India clamoring for progress, jobs and material things - and the softer, dimmer voices of the old India calling for simplicity, and return to the "inner light." I found both views inspiring and incredibly invigorating while living in India. But I was mostly glad that there is still such a place where inner light shines, and those dim voices continue.

The Jewel on the Hand

ॐ

I was traveling in Mumbai on business one day in the Fall, during the great festival of the chubby elephant headed deity, Ganesh. During this festival season, millions of clay statues in various sizes and ornamentation are created and purchased by the devotees of Ganesh. After offering puja and parading the statues around the city in procession, the statues are submerged in the rivers and ocean. The imagery of the gods going back to earth and joining in the life cycle as they become mud again offers a compelling view of the Hindu view of rebirth, and "the chakra", or wheel of life. The airport was crowded that particular day, and Mumbai, India's most cosmopolitan city, was jammed with its usual procession of travelers, many of whom were no doubt there for the festival.

I was in line at the airport ticket counter and a middle aged Indian man put his hand on my shoulder and asked me "are you having good luck with that ring?" He pointed to my right hand, where I had a simple gold ring with a sapphire stone mounted on it. I had purchased the ring in Bangalore only a few months before. He began again to inquire as to my "luck," and then began to speak of the power of the stone itself. He told me that the rather dark blue sapphire gem could bring very good luck, or very bad luck. I told him, sort of jokingly, that so far everything was great, I enjoyed the ring, being in India, and my luck was fine! He proceeded on to his flight. The episode got me thinking about the Indian belief in gems and astrology, and their sacred powers of healing, and their ability to play an important role in that store of luck, good or bad, in one's life.

Shortly after I arrived in India, I noticed the fascination with jewelry, and the exotic beauty and craftsmanship of the women's jewels in particular. While bangles of all sorts are readily available, and worn as day to day decoration by almost every woman in India, bridal jewelry is probably the most ornate and spectacular of all. I can still see the huge billboards on MG Road in Bangalore advertising "Krishnachetty Jewelers," with a beautiful Indian bride modeling amazing gold creations for the neck, nose, ears, forehead, and hair. In India, almost every aspect of the body, down to the ankles and toes, has a piece of jewelry appropriate for that part of the body. I had heard that in many cases a woman's jewels represented her own individual wealth, her personal wealth, and as such jewelry was desired both for ornamentation and its financial value. I was trying to reconcile this with the Hindu views of sacrifice and renunciation.

What I found more interesting, however, were the rings worn by the men in India. This is because many Indian men wear multiple rings, and almost all shared the same pattern, finger placement, and color scheme on the individual fingers. I recall often seeing a green stone on the pinky, a red stone on the traditional ring finger, a blue stone, like my sapphire, on the middle finger, and a white or transparent "moon" stone on the index finger. My colleagues and co-workers, people I met in the bank, and even laborers or drivers would typically have some combination of these stones on their hand. Of course, non-precious metals could easily substitute for gold, and costume gem stones or colored glass would substitute for emeralds, sapphires, or rubies. But what was the meaning behind this combination of jewels?

According to the website of the Vedic Cultural Fellowship (http://www.vedicworld.org/vedic_astrology/) a person's birth date, birth time and birth place can be used to create a horoscope in Indian astrology. The major precious stones correspond to different temperaments and energies locked in the planets and in their rotations. A skilled astrologer of the Vedas can study these horoscopes and planetary alignments, and determine the appropriate gems that will positively influence the person's luck, or prospects in life. According to the Vedic Cultural Fellowship, the "gems that a person can wear all throughout their lives can bolster their physical health, calm and focus their minds, or attract certain influences towards the person in greater measure. The horoscope is studied from the perspective of all 9 of the major gems used and corresponding to the 7 major planets and 2 nodes of the Moon. By strengthening planets that can increase gains in life, you can gain results in greater measure. This is true whether you are trying to improve health, communications, relationships, find greater success in your careers or businesses, or even further your spiritual proclivities. "Wow. !!! See website, above.

I now understood why the gentleman in Mumbai asked me about my sapphire ring. I purchased a green emerald as well, hoping to tap into some more of the cosmic good stuff! So did my brother in law and neighbor, when I told them about the positive qualities. My brother in law lost his ring after visiting India. That was bad luck. He found it again about 18 months later. Good luck! What kind of luck will he have in the future?

When you question an Indian about these stones and their powers or about astrology in general, you find out that very few important dates, like a wedding or the opening of a new business, are made without ascertaining the "right time" from an astrologer. Many people in India will be firmly devoted to these ancient practices and the wisdom contained therein. Others will respect the fact that many believe in the powers of astrology and gems, and will argue that it can't hurt to follow the guidance of the astrologers, as it has been practiced for a long time. Others, although not many that I met, will scoff at the practices as superstitious, but will still readily go along with the guidance of an astrologer if convenient, "just in case."

My particular motivation in the purchase of my rings, other than in their souvenir value, was a lasting connection to the people, beliefs and crafts of India. Many view the gemstones as powerful devices which can help believers, and non-believers improve their lives. Much of this impressed me as consistent with so many religious beliefs that I encountered in India. People generally respected what was holy, whether or not they followed the philosophies or spiritual directives of a particular sect or group. The point was that there was likely enough evidence that seeking blessings from a holy source was good in and of itself, and you could gain the benefits of such blessings by, for example, wearing the right color ring on the right finger!

I wear both my blue and green rings almost every day. I don't really think of any connection with the celestial orbs, or the channeling of some needed cosmic energy to improve my life as I wear them. People will frequently ask me about the rings, and it will serve as an opening for a discussion on my experiences in India, and some very special people and times that I cherish.

However, in true Indian fashion, I'm equally open to soaking up some planetary cosmic rays channeling through these rings to improve my luck in life!

The Swami

ॐ

One morning, shortly after my arrival in Bangalore, I met some Americans of Indian origin at my hotel near MG Road. We were at breakfast on the buffet line, and as it was a bit crowded, I did not want to take a table just for myself. I asked if I could join the small group of guests I had just met, as they had two extra seats at their table. Over coffee, masala dosa, and some fresh mango slices with yoghurt, we began to talk about our reasons for being in Bangalore.

The hotels were packed at this time, and it was hard for me to even book a room in advance for my trip. Bangalore was becoming a "hot" destination. My story was likely similar to the majority of visitors, as many IT and professional foreigners were invading Bangalore for work. My breakfast guests, however, had come to India in search of spiritual enlightenment! As I was only a few days in India, I started thinking of the Beatles, their time in Rishikesh, and gurus, swamis, and hippies! I was a bit skeptical, and perhaps a bit surprised about their stated mission, as I was focused on the corporate world, finding my office, and trying to project an image of confidence to mask my underlying fear of this new place!

That chance meeting at breakfast became my first introduction to the spiritual core of India - the search for God inside oneself, and the Hindu tradition of approaching God through the study of Vedanta. The word Vedanta comes from two words, "veda," Sanskrit for "knowledge," and "anta," Sanskrit for "the end." I was sitting at breakfast preparing to work as a lawyer in India focusing on technology and software. And I was surrounded by 4 intelligent young people who had come to India to study the eternal principles of life and living, the "end of knowledge." The goal of the Vendanta philosophy is "self-realization." I was fascinated that these two extremes could coexist on my first day in India, at least at the same breakfast table among strangers! I became interested in learning more about this ancient knowledge.

There was something so warm, open and welcoming about these people I had just met. As I got up to go to work, they heartily bid me farewell, said that they hoped we would meet again at the hotel, and told me that they had some important gathering in Bangalore for their school that very evening. I was intrigued, but didn't have enough time to get their full story. However, at lunch time, I had to make a trip into town to change some money. There in line were the same students, happily chatting away despite the crowd and the heat. They immediately came over, and as the line was long, began to tell me about their teacher who was visiting Bangalore from their Vedanta Academy in Mumbai. They invited me to join them that evening at the Bangalore Town Hall, where Swami Parthasarathy was giving a lecture on Vedantic studies.

I could hear in the background "Young grasshopper, when the student is ready, the teacher will appear!"

A little more about Vedanta. According to Swami Parthasarathy, the study of Vedanta is the study of capturing the highest thoughts of humanity, to answer the fundamental and eternal questions of life, and thereby improve spiritual and, interestingly, material well being. It is the road to the Real Self, which is inside each of us, and the Real Self is divine. Finding it, by uncluttering one's life through meditation, detachment, renunciation, and concentration, will lead to bliss. Finding the Real Self is not an experience or event that takes us by surprise, at a moment of cosmic enlightenment, as in movies. There is no walking in the hills, only to be struck by divine light, with the "ah ha!" moment. Rather, Vedantic studies train the student to get inside the real essence of one's life, to put aside worldly views thrust upon us by the media, or opinions which we value because we think others find them important. Vedanta teaches self discipline and truly independent thinking.

Contrary to what we think about "things "making us happy in the West, at the core of the Vedanta discipline is learning that "desire for anything increases restriction and prohibition." Thus Vedanta does not contain the typical lists of do's and don'ts found in many religions. It is intended to liberate one's mind, to unclutter it from outside influences, and to find the soul, deep inside ourselves, where God dwells. According to Vedanta, the answers are inside us if we are quiet enough, and observant enough, to listen.

Because of this strong appeal, Vedanta academies have grown in number throughout India and the world. Vedanta is a course of study, with practices like meditation and yoga, to put aside the tensions and traps of materialism and desire. Swami Parthasarathy declares "Living is an art, a skill, a technique. You need to learn the technique of living and practice it as you would a musical instrument" Thus students who are really in search of these eternal truths will move to the Vedanta academies and undertake several years of study and practice. The Vedanta academies can be modern looking schools with well appointed campuses, or they can resemble more simple, austere, ashrams. At the Vedanta Academy in Pune, a city near Mumbai, students are offered a three year, full time, residential course, regardless of nationality or religion. Courses are taught in English, with an emphasis on Sanskrit, in order to capture the original spiritual texts (the Vedas) and facilitate participation in chanting and praying the Vedas. Because the course encourages different approaches to finding one's Self, literature and poetry are used to supplement the teachings.

I felt blessed, even on day three, to be in a country where people still seek out this knowledge. Mahatma Gandhi said that India's special relationship to humanity is to be the spiritual compass in a world lost in war and selfish living. Where else, other than India, would 20 year olds, and corporate executives alike, wake up at 4:15am for prayer and study, followed by Yoga and jogging, then breakfast at 8:30am, with classes, yard work around the campus to keep it in good shape, followed by meditation, rest, dinner and retiring at 9pm? This is the basic curriculum of the Vedanta school. The classroom emphasis is on the three traditional spiritual disciplines of karma (which means "action"); bhakti (devotion), and jhana (knowledge). In some cases, given the widespread interest in Vedantic studies in India, a patron who sponsors a student for such coursework may receive a tax deduction!

At the invitation of the young people I had met, I attended the lecture, or better stated, celebration, that evening. All the students were dressed in white robes and were hurrying into the Town Hall, which had Swami Parthasarathy's kindly face emblazoned on a 40 foot long banner across the front. I guess some amount of advertising is ok, as long as it seeks to promote knowledge of the inner self!

From inside came the sound of chanting, praying and light music. There was a tremendous feeling of lightness and joy in the room, which was filled to capacity by at least 1000 people. For those, like me, not skilled in Sanskrit, there were English phonetic transcriptions of the Sanskrit words on an overhead projector so that all could join in. I sat down near the front, to increase the likelihood that something good would sink in, and found myself next to a very kindly older gentleman who lived in Bangalore. He had come to the evening event alone, as had I.

We began talking about our interest in these kinds of lectures, and he told me about his son, off living in the US, and working for a software company. There was certain sadness in his story, and I could sense he was a bit lonely, although he smiled most of the time as we spoke. I was making the opposite trip, coming to India for work in the software industry. He said to me, "We should get together for coffee and talk again sometime." At that time, having newly arrived in India, I didn't even have a cell phone or a permanent address yet, as I was still staying in the hotel. He gave me his phone number. I'm sure it got lost over the next several weeks as I began moving into my normal pace of life. I should have called him, but things got busy for me. Maybe the teacher was sitting next to me and I didn't know it? In a strange twist, I found his phone number recently stuck between the pages of a book on Vedanta.

Towards the end of the evening's presentations, I began to learn that Swami Parthasarahy was a pretty important instructor in the Vedanta world, and in fact lectured frequently all over the world, even at corporate meetings and other gatherings. I stood in line to buy his book. It is called "The Eternities – Vedanta Treatise" by A. Parthasarathy, which I highly recommend for an open minded individual seeking to tap into the ways that Eastern thought approaches life and the world. At that moment, the students that I had met earlier in the day came running over to me, made a bit of a fuss to Swami-ji about me, being an American, working here, and what a "good guy" I was for coming that evening. How did they come to that conclusion from our breakfast discussion? Was it simply because I was interested in Vedanta? Could they sense that there was something more that I was destined to learn in India? Swami welcomed me, and thanked me for coming. Despite the long line of many devotees behind me, he took time to tell me about his travels in the US, and the many lectures he had given throughout the country. He signed his book for me, dated Nov. 5th, 2005, with my own pen, which I now believe is mightier then the sword!

Inside the book, Swami-ji's handwritten phrase summarized Vedantic teaching. "Discover Thy Self." What a fascinating journey India was to be for me!

A piece of Goa

ॐ

I was traveling in Goa with friends, and noticed an old house being renovated. The old homes in Goa do not resemble the British style "bungalows" of Dehli or Bangalore, because the British influence never really took root in Goa. Goa's European influence came from Portugal, and the Goan homes have a more Mediterranean feel, with pretty wood carvings reminiscent of Christian church doors and, lots of floral designs and tile work. However, like the British bungalows, the older single family homes of Goa are largely in need of significant repair, and the materials, skill and labor to preserve them are costly. Many such structures sit all but abandoned, with only a hint of their former lovely painted exteriors, bright yellows, greens and reds, barely visible.

Generally the owners of these big homes are living elsewhere, waiting to sell the plot to investors, knowing that the homes will likely be torn down. Few have the money to keep up the historical look of the houses. Homes in Goa tend to have a bit of land and lots of natural beauty, and I met several tourists in

Goa in the process of buying property there. In the south part of the province, near Mobar, and Cavalossim, the atmosphere is particularly quiet, with little traffic, and feels tropical. It is very different from normal city life in India, and one can see why this is a popular place to travel for relaxation. I would say that even the clothing style is a bit different from the rest of India, inasmuch as Christian women are more likely to wear European style skirts or dresses, instead of saris and salwar chameez.

This particular old house was in a small compound, off the main road, which was hardly more then a 2 lane, relatively quiet, access road to the southern resorts. Names like Dona Sylvia's, and Garofino's let the tourist know that he or she is not really in "mainstream" India. It turns out that some friends knew the owner of the house, and around the yard were haphazard heaps of building materials, a dog, and the remnants of an old well. In a corner I spotted some beautifully carved pieces of a patio decoration that were completely worn down to the wood, in some cases worm eaten, although some traces of their once colorful painting could be seen. They were certainly hand carved, and seemed to form a border around the patio or porch. All but about four pieces had significant dry rot, and were being thrown out by the owner. I was intrigued at the history of these wooden pieces, the fact that they were a part of Goa's separate and unique history. What hands might have carved them over 100 years ago? What was this part of the country like then? Was Portuguese the dominant language then? Was this a part of some larger mansion, that had imported European laborers working on the house for a wealthy Goan? I decided to ask the owner if I could take the 4 intact pieces back to Bangalore with me. She said of course, and back they came after a good deal of wrapping and careful packaging.

I gave two pieces to a friend who was equally intrigued, and then brought the other two pieces back to the US with my belongings. While I was in Goa, I also found a very strange seed, about the size of a silver dollar, which I picked up and have to this day. It is too dried out to plant, but I wonder if this was a sacred banyan tree seed, or some other exotic tree like mango? I have no idea, and yet somehow I keep it around, on my desk, on a table, just around, to remind me of how the world is full of beginnings, and interesting possibilities and hope.

Eventually I cleaned off these pieces of wood, painted them as best I could using the traces of paint that I could still see as a guide, and hung them up on a wall in my house. People ask me all the time where such interesting pieces came from, what was their history, and how nice it must be to have this piece of real history in my house.

I look at these relics and see Indian woods, hand crafted by skilled laborers in this unique part of Goa, a hundred years ago, for a wealthy individual whose history remains unknown to me. This history now sits in my house in Connecticut, on a wall built by Latin American laborers, next to a picture of Norway. I can smell the salt, the palms, and feel the history in these pieces of wood. And I feel the interconnectedness of our small world.

Departure

ॐ

I headed into the office on my last day in India. My visa would
expire the next day, I had all my things packed, and the movers had
removed all the contents of my apartment several days before. As
I left the place I had lived in for two years, many of the workers,
those who had clipped the grass, and cleaned the common areas,
seemed to delay their activities as I got into my car for the last
time. I imagine that the commotion caused by the moving of my
goods days before spoke to the fact that change was happening.
I did give a good deal of my Indian household goods to those
who had helped me the most over my two years. For us in the
West, the comings and goings of people and events happen so
quickly that we hardly take notice. For many of these workers in
Bangalore, most of whom came from rural backgrounds where
life's patterns are the same and predictable, the emptying of an
apartment was a bit of an event.

I remember handing my keys to one of the young guards at
the lobby level. He said to me "leaving, sir?" When I told him yes,
he immediately shot back "When are you coming back to India?"

I did not know the answer to that question, but I do know what I wanted it to be. Soooooooon! Walking out the door, I got the last salute from a friendly security guard as he held the door open since my hands were full. His smile and shake of the head gave me both a sad and joyful feeling inside. Perhaps it was the Hindu detachment, the lack of emotion, and the constant, completeness of his gaze and smile. It is hard to say goodbye sometimes, even to people you didn't know well, when their constant and steady presence represents many days, weeks and months of memories.

Arriving at work, my co-workers seemed quieter then normal. Generally, I always noticed how much livelier our Indian offices were then those back in headquarters. People took time to interact, to laugh, with dueling phone conversations getting progressively louder. Workers would take coffee together for a few minutes and catch up on work, and few thought twice about shouting across the floor to a worker on the other side if something was needed. That morning my co-workers knew that I would not be returning, and they told me how much I was valued as a co-worker and a friend. In addition to working together, we had joined up to play some music, traded songs and guitar lessons over the two years, and had shared many jokes, meals and the ups and downs of office life. Plus, we both got insight into each other's world and views.

A little going away gathering was soon underway with soft drinks, cake, and some Indian food, which was able to break the bittersweet sense of departure that was welling up inside me. As I looked at these faces, and began to answer questions about what I'd be doing back in the US, would I be coming back, "will you remember us Bob?", can we sing that song again together, we will miss you," I began to feel that I had successfully completed both a work assignment, and a personal transformation. I received as a going away gift a beautifully hand carved family of elephants, all marching together, and the team joked that I was the "big" elephant, and they were following me. They told me that they had learned so much about how the Corporation worked, had gained career insight, and hoped that I would always put in a good word for them, some of whom wished to complete assignments in the US.

But the greatest complement of all was from the non-management workers with whom I had spent a good deal of time simply interacting, day in and day out. One guy told me "Bob, you are more Indian then we are, you know more about India then we do! We never had a foreigner here who embraced our culture as much as you. "Another said to me, "you are the only one of the assignees from headquarters that we could feel completely comfortable with … we didn't need to change our style because of you. "I was flattered to hear that I hadn't caused these friends to feel that they needed to be on guard when a senior manager from corporate headquarters was in their midst. I had always tried to work within the context and milieu of my colleagues. I did not "hold my breath" while I was in India. With that, I felt a certain completeness and peacefulness, and was ready to return home and resume my life in the US.

I had been invited to a friend's house for dinner that evening, as I no longer had my apartment, and my flight did not depart until 1:30am. I enjoyed my last locally prepared Indian meal, and we celebrated a bit with a few large Kingfisher beers in the living room while talking, and with some Bollywood movie on the TV in the background. At one point in the conversation a rat scurried across the floor and ran into the kitchen. My friend's wife and daughter were already upstairs sleeping, and my friend said to me, completely calmly, with a smile on his face, "Did you see that? Should we try and get it out?" I looked at him and burst out loud laughing. The rat went behind the refrigerator, and my last official act in India was to catch the rat in a bucket as my friend shoved a broom behind the fridge. Once captured, he took the rat outside into his yard and let it go. There was no attempt to kill it. He just said to me that there must be a hole somewhere in the foundation, which he would have to fix. Talk about detachment! It was as if a moth had simply flown in through the window.

It was getting late, and I needed to get to the airport, so I called my driver Harish for the last time, and asked him to wait outside. I said goodbye to my friend, who, because of his role in the company, I would thankfully see again. It was a great relaxing evening, and the beer took the edge off the mosquitoes that I would certainly encounter in the waiting room at the airport.

We passed the many familiar buildings, streets and signs quite quickly, as it was after midnight and the roads were generally clear. I was holding back a tear, and was glad when I saw a cow on the side of the road to break up the silence. It may have been the same one that greeted me when I arrived two years earlier! I was especially sad to say goodbye to Harish, and I told him how much I appreciated his service, and that I would give him any reference that he wanted.

It was not easy to walk into the airport, but the chaos of the Bangalore gates and check in process brought me back to reality. It was really over.

Epilogue - Since My Return

ॐ

I have been back from India for 2 years now. I'm still corresponding with many of my former clients in India, since we continue to work for the same company, and thankfully I'm still in touch with many friends in Bangalore. In my free time, I try to keep up with Hindi and use it whenever I can with Indians that I meet here in the US. The reaction I get remains positive, which gives me confidence, so I'll keep going until I run out of materials, or the reaction gets worse! I do want to tackle the Hindi script at some point in time, and will add this to a growing list of retirement activities that will keep me from annoying my family and friends when I have too much time on my hands.

I continue to crave Indian food, requiring it about once a week. I've taken to buying the pre-made breads, parathas and naan's, as well as vegetarian dishes like mutter paneer, dal makhani and various aloo (potato) dishes that are easily found in a local Indian market. It is funny how 2 minutes in the microwave can transport me 10,000 miles back to those wonderful meals that I ate everyday, and have come to love. I recently found a can of "jackfruit" at an Indian market near my house, and I find myself thinking about taking an Indian food cooking class somewhere at a community education course. I watch Hindi movies when I can, still with subtitles, and continue to subject friends and family to several of my personal favorites, including "Rang de Basanti" and the "Munna Bhai" series I mentioned earlier, and of course the "Gandhi" epic with Ben Kingsley.

I'm increasingly drawn to the many books on India that I purchased from the used bookseller on Church Street in Bangalore. Occasionally a name, number, or clipping falls from the pages which brings me back in time to a particular moment or event. I have now read my favorite book, "Freedom at Midnight", by Dominique LaPierre, twice since I've been back. The book treats the history of India's Partition, and many other topics of religion, culture and history. I give copies of LaPierre's "City of Joy" to almost anyone who is interested, and have started to devote an entire bookshelf to the dozens of volumes in my collection that deal, even tangentially, with India in some way.

During the summer time I can wear my kurtas (loose Indian shirts), and tee shirts from India. My favorite is still a simple shirt that has the symbols of Hinduism, Christianity, Judaism, Buddhims, Islam and Jainism across the front, with the words "God is too big to fit into one religion" across the bottom. I still wear the shirt with my name, and "Bangaluru", written in the squiggly Kannada script whenever I can, and generally dress up in my Indian wedding clothes at Halloween. It is not because I think the clothes are scary, or even funny. I guess Halloween is about the only time I can pull it off and walk comfortably down the street. The first time I wore the Indian wedding garb, my son and his friends had knocked on the door of some neighbors down the street for "trick or treat". The owners happened to be Indian, and an older Indian woman, herself dressed in salwar chameez, spotted me in the background with my Congress party khadi hat, and starting gesturing and quickly speaking Gujarati to me. I had no idea what she was saying, but I felt very at home and really had a good laugh when her son pulled her back inside the house, trying to explain Halloween to her.

I find myself opening up my photo albums all the time, to anyone who takes the slightest interest in my trip, and I constantly print out pictures that I can hang on my wall in the office. I use a pen I bought at one of the handicraft cooperatives in Bangalore. I still prefer my Hindustan Machines Tool (HMT) wrist watch, which I bought for $5 dollars from a vendor in Pondicherry, to other more up to date and expensive timepieces. My Hero bicycle is still in the garage, and not really up to the hills of Danbury, Connecticut, but it does get dusted off and the tires are pumped up frequently. Our house is adorned with the beautiful wooden inlaid scenes of village life in India, as well as the carpets which spent their first two years on the marble floors of my flat in Bangalore. I frequently check out the on-line version of "India Today" magazine to see what is happening locally, and I go out of my way at work to find Indian's that I can share my experience with. I hope they don't grow tired of my tedious questions and efforts to practice Hindi with them.

Several months back, a priest from Bangalore arrived at one of the neighboring parishes for the summer. I could hardly wait to contact him and have lunch, and catch up on what was going on in Bangalore. He told me about the progress of the metro down MG Road, the recent goings on in the community, and about the chapel I used to visit. We talked about places we both knew, about restaurants we have both dined in, about market areas, cultural differences. He drives a scooter, and I shared with him that I had just purchased a moped, made in India, which I dart around town on in good weather. He invited me to Bangalore anytime, and I'm sure I will take him up on it.

Travel always challenges us, and improves us if we are open to differences. Living in another country forces us to exhale, to open our lungs and minds and hearts to different points of view.

When you try to understand why people are the way they are, or why a country is the "way it is", you stop asking questions like "why this place is dirty, "or" why is there such poverty?" You begin to ask about the potential for the country and its people, and you begin to thank God for the diversity he has given us, for the different points of view in our world, for the many holy and good paths which lead to Him. And I can still chuckle about rickshaws and rickshaw drivers, and marvel at structures like the Taj Mahal. And perhaps most importantly, I think about a land where some people would go without clothing as a sign of their complete dependence on God, and be honored for the holy path they had chosen.

I can think of no other place in the world like India. Like the current travel advertisements state, India is "ananya".. sanksrit for "like no other." India is where "made by hand" is the norm, where religious symbols are a part of the workplace and shops, and where a hot meal of vegetables, spices and fresh bread is standard. Most importantly, I think about the incredible spirit of the people I met, and what motivates them, despite their challenges, to move forward.

What a wonderful conversation it has been with India. I am grateful for all that I was privileged enough to experience. This kind of experience doesn't happen everywhere. It happens in India because its people see God in everything, and especially in the visitor. The Guest is God.

I'll have another cup of chai on the crowded streets anyday. I hope the conversation never ends.

The faces of India's future

The author near the Nepal border in Darjeeling